PRAISE FOR

Prayer and You:
Wit and Wisdom from a Crabby Mystic

"Afraid of praying? Confused about how to pray? Wondering where to begin? Sister Mary Lea Hill's warm and witty book on prayer is like sitting down with an experienced spiritual director who has a great sense of humor. Let her invite you, in ways that are by turns provocative, lighthearted and profound, into a deeper relationship with the God who desires to be in relationship with you."

> — James Martin, SJ, author of
> *The Jesuit Guide to (Almost) Everything*

"Step away from your preconceived notions and prepare yourself to be delighted and challenged in equal measure. Sister Lea Hill raises the bar on prayer books for normal people. *Prayer and You* is sure to be a book you dog-ear, highlight, share, and, most importantly, put into practice."

> — Sarah Reinhard, author of *Catholic Family Fun*

"If you've ever struggled in prayer or wished for a better prayer life (and most of us probably have at one time or another), then this book is for you. Sister Mary Lea Hill's insights about prayer draw on the rich traditions of the Church, while presenting a practical way for the reader to grow spiritually in today's world. That's an achievement in itself, but Sister Lea also manages to be humorous as she shares her wisdom! *Prayer and You* is a great resource for Catholics looking for ways to unite more deeply with God through their daily life of prayer."

— Timothy Michael Cardinal Dolan, Archbishop of New York

Prayer and You

Prayer and You

Wit and Wisdom
from a Crabby Mystic

Mary Lea Hill, FSP

auline
BOOKS & MEDIA
Boston

Library of Congress Cataloging-in-Publication Data

Hill, Mary Lea.
  Prayer and you : wit and wisdom from a crabby mystic / Mary Lea Hill, FSP.
    pages cm
  Includes index.
  ISBN-13: 978-0-8198-5999-0
  ISBN-10: 0-8198-5999-0
  1. Prayer--Catholic Church. 2. Spiritual life--Catholic Church. 3. Catholic Church--
Doctrines. I. Title.
  BV210.3.H558 2014
  248.3'2--dc23

2013046680

Cover design by Rosana Usselmann

Cover photo: © istockphoto.com/ horiyan and rrocio

Published by Pauline Books & Media, 50 Saint Pauls Avenue, Boston, MA 02130-3491

Printed in the U.S.A.

www.pauline.org

Pauline Books & Media is the publishing house of the Daughters of St. Paul, an international congregation of women religious serving the Church with the communications media.

2 3 4 5 6 7 8 9   20 19 18 17 16 15

For all who struggle with prayer

Contents ~~~~~~~~~~~~~~~~~~~~~~~~~~~~~~~~~~~~

Introduction

This is a book about you.

Did you think it was about prayer?

I'm willing to bet that many people pick it up because it says right on the cover that it's for *you*. You, however, may have picked it up because it says it's about prayer—there is no argument here. Truthfully, prayer is about you. Even more so, we can say that prayer *is* you. Prayer doesn't exist aside from the pray-er. The Church's liturgy is prayer that gathers us together. There are books of prayer, hundreds of them. But without pray-ers, these prayers are only ink on paper or data in an electronic device. You, and only you, are prayer.

Do we need to be taught to pray? Yes and no. As members of the most intelligent species on earth we are natural pray-ers. Why do we say this? The reason is obvious: we were born to communicate. By nature we are communicators, and prayer is communication.

Still, we may feel the need of some direction in prayer. Who do we pray to? What do we say? Why? When? Where? Is it better to pray one-on-one or as a group? Can prayer be done badly? Does it always work? We may have endless concerns and questions.

I hope that this book will help you as you begin to pray, as you become a pray-er. It is not an instructional course on prayer, but rather a taster on prayer, a place to get your feet wet. It could also be called a starter kit although it has no parts, no how-to directions, just a random set of suggestions on prayer. I recommend reading them casually, then thoughtfully, and then again prayerfully. As you do this, I hope you will discover the natural ebb and flow of your own prayerfulness. And in the busy-ness of your days, may you find yourself seeking opportunities to slip into a moment or two of prayer.

Can a Swear Be a Prayer?

Prayer

Can a swear be a prayer? Here I have to draw a line, but not where you may be thinking. My line, of course, cuts off those expressions that are rude, crude, and uncouth. However, what will we say of the superabundant OMGs that fill the air around us? If an indulgence was attached to every OMG in the world of texting, for example, grace would superabound.

Historically, many favorite Catholic prayers begin with those same three words, *O my God!* They are certainly said with some intention of a "real" prayer, but what about the random everyday use?

Perhaps most of us have uttered a sudden, unplanned "O my God!" out of fright, or surprise, or some kind of shock. Do you automatically clap a hand over your mouth when you realize that you have just used God's name in vain, as the second commandment says? But is it really "in vain," useless, or offensive to call out to God even so unconsciously?

We all know when we have purposely been disrespectful, when we "*dis*" someone. Are these careless OMGs cases of disrespect toward God? I suggest that they are not, but that they are real prayers arising from the heart. They are the Holy Spirit reminding us of our need for God. He is speaking a prayer from within us.

> *Likewise the Spirit also helps us in our weakness, for we don't know how to pray as we should; instead, the Spirit himself pleads for us with inexpressive groanings, and the One who is able to see what's in the heart knows what the Spirit wishes, because the Spirit intercedes for the saints in accordance with God's will. (Rm 8:26–27)*

And you

Thank the Spirit for calling out from your heart. Make a point of being more aware of and at home with God's presence within you. It could become your practice to consciously offer up as a prayer every offhand use of God's name that you hear: yours or those of others.

Ho-Hum Prayer

Prayer

Has the thought crossed your mind that prayer is really a waste of time? Does the mere suggestion of prayer call forth your most emphatic "ho-hum"? Perhaps you see prayer as something to put off for old age or a practice to be entrusted to a more pious relative. Do you prefer to do something useful or entertaining? Of course we have other things to attend to, for example, study. We understand the importance of study for passing tests and earning good grades. Work is necessary in order to gain the livelihood to support ourselves and those we love. And it provides a feeling of self-worth. This goes for all types of work. Working the soil, or even just the front lawn, is likewise an obvious need. Farmers and pickers provide the variety of produce we expect in our grocery stores. Just one look at our own little backyard gardens reminds us that the harvest requires lots of time and attention. But prayer? What does prayer produce? Does it irk your pride to ask for something rather than work for it? If so, be consoled because actually prayer *is* work, and it demands a lot more from us than we are willing to admit. Prayer, in fact, *is* us: my prayer is me! The main concern is not so much the prayer as the pray-er.

> *Don't deceive yourselves! If any of you think you're wise in this age, become foolish, so you'll be truly wise. (1 Cor 3:18)*

And you

If you haven't dipped a toe into prayer lately, remove those work shoes and just go for it. What to say? Try this: *I haven't been by much, Lord, but I thought I'd drop in today just to say hello, and thanks, too.* There, that was simple. You just prayed. You are a pray-er. Keep it up!

3

A Nod to Prayer

Prayer

"Oh, I can't possibly. I'm so tired!" Have you ever heard yourself utter these words when invited to drop by church after work for the rosary or a novena? And what about a few minutes for night prayer before retiring?

Now imagine what you will be doing with that half-hour or those few minutes you cannot spare. "But I really am tired," you say. Of course you are tired from a day of working or even studying. You should be tired. But does life end because we are tired? No, we come home and *make* supper, *pick up* the kids, *walk* the dog, *clean* the dishes, *straighten* and *dust*, *pay* some bills, *prepare* for tomorrow, and so much more. After that you are even more tired. Welcome to your very normal life!

"I really do need a couple minutes to relax!" Very true and understandable, but how will you relax? Some sports on TV? (Suppose your team is losing?) A little Internet or the daily paper? (Even the urgency of the ads is nerve-racking.) Play a computer game? (If you're competitive this won't be relaxing either.) And so, if your only option is to sit there and stare, you might as well give a nod to prayer. Nothing fancy. No books. Forget your posture, just relax. "What if I fall asleep?" you gasp.

It's not that you stuck your padded purse, or not-so-padded wallet, under your head for a comforting snooze. We are really no more responsible for falling asleep than for simply falling as we walk. Of course, no one intentionally sets out to be an accident waiting to happen. It just happens. So it is when we nod in prayer. The one very good thing it says about us is that we are comfortable in God's presence. If anyone understands why we are tired, it is God. And he loves us for it. So sit back for a couple of minutes and tell God how your day went, ask a question, ask a favor. Or perhaps just sit and look at God with love.

And he said to them, "Come away privately, just yourselves, to a desert place and rest for a bit." (Mk 6:31)

And you

If you can spare a moment, sit down now. Take a long, relaxing breath or two. Give your attention to God and begin, perhaps with a "help me" or a "thank you."

4

The Pi of Prayer

Prayer

For thousands of years people have been trying to unravel the mystery of Pi. Someone did find that the circumference of a circle divided by the diameter would produce a ratio, but that ratio is very hard to nail down. It doesn't work out in any definite number, but any circle will result in exactly the same number as every other circle, no matter the size. Puzzled? You have every right to be. It's a little irrational. The most definite thing that can be said is that the mystery of Pi is transcendental, or, more simply put, pretty impossible to figure out.

We have a lot of these transcendental teachings in our religion, for example, the Trinity, the Incarnation, the Eucharist, the Resurrection. They are the eternal puzzles of our faith. Here we need to take our cue from mathematicians. They grab hold of some intellectual mystery, prove to themselves that it is beyond their collective abilities, and then simply enjoy its beauty. A mathematician will sit down surrounded by numbers and compute off into the sunset, content in the process, enjoying the search.

When we approach our sacred mysteries in prayer, we come in that same spirit of joyful pursuit. Will we ever discover the inner secrets of the Trinity? Or figure out how God became man? And is there a proof that bread and wine actually become the Body and Blood of Jesus Christ? What about our belief that Jesus rose alive after three days in the grave? So the best way to address these mysteries in prayer is to savor the mystery. Be grateful that there is something beyond us. God and his mysteries are perfection. We are not, but we can still find our joy in simple contemplation.

Instead we preach God's wisdom, a wisdom which is secret and hidden and which God ordained before the ages for our glory. (1 Cor 2:7)

And you

Rather than tying your imagination in knots attempting to understand the mysteries of God, spend some quality time praising his wisdom. God loves the attention. So don't be afraid to simply admire his Beauty, Truth, and Goodness.

5

A Way in a Manger

Prayer

Every Christmas we gaze at lovely manger scenes and listen to lilting Christmas hymns. Perhaps we offer a prayer of thanks that neither we nor our children had to be born in such poverty. Yet we know that countless women around the world give birth in circumstances similar to Bethlehem's stable, or even worse. How many fathers must try to shelter their spouses from worry over the precarious situation of their little families? However, as much as such images move us, right now we are selfishly concentrating on our own prayer life.

The sweet music of Christmas includes the beloved hymn, "Away in a Manger." May I suggest that we seek for ourselves *a way in a manger*? Our prayer life, both our contemplation and our lived prayer, finds a model in the manger. Poverty, simplicity, dependence, hospitality, mortification, transparency, and so many other virtues flow from the lovely scene before us.

We picture Mary's tenderness, Joseph's attentiveness. Neighbors and strangers come to visit him while angels adore him. That first Christmas was all about the baby. We would do well to reconnect with our inner self and rediscover the purity, simplicity, and dependence we should have before our God.

Before the manger, we learn how God feels about life. Just as at the first Bethlehem, we imagine the prickly straw, the odor of animals, and the chill wind of life to accept with the innocence of a child. The manger gives us a lesson on how to pare down our necessities a little closer to the essential. The story of the first Christmas is also a vivid study in compassion. If we allow our thoughts and prayers to dwell on the scene we will notice many opportunities to live the spirit of Christmas in daily life.

> *She gave birth to her first born son, wrapped him in swaddling clothes, and laid him in a manger, because there was no room for them in the inn. (Lk 2:7)*

And you

Let your heart simmer in a little tenderness. Think of the sweetness, the innocence, the helplessness of a newborn. Wrap your soul around the scene. Ask yourself: Is my soul impoverished and destitute or does it mirror the true spirit of Christmas? Do I live humbly, simply?

6

Bargain Basement Prayer

Prayer

We sometimes scramble around in our prayer as if we were in a big-name bargain basement. At these sales-havens we can discover coveted merchandise and outrageous deals after only minutes of searching. But prayer doesn't work like that, does it? Whatever answer we receive in prayer, it is a gift. God owes us nothing, not even what we have already received.

Praying is more like Christmas than like shopping. God is ever watchful—vigilant as any loving parent awaiting the child's every need. We are constantly being gifted, and we call these gifts grace.

My family recently discovered some "Dear Santa" letters my father wrote nearly a century ago. One year he wrote out his list only to replace it several days later with another in which he pleads for a train set to share with his brother. He dutifully tacked on neckties and school books as well. As a courtesy, cookies and cocoa would be waiting for jolly Saint Nick.

When we pray as grown-ups, we may find that some things seem to be crossed off our "Dear God" letter. Are we loved less than before? No. But our Father wants us to receive bigger, more valuable gifts than those we can think of on our own. "What gifts?" we ask. *The outrageous blessings of faith, hope, love, patience, perseverance, and anticipation.* For these we needn't wait for Christmas. We can receive them any-where, at any time. These gifts distinguish an adult Christian from an innocent little kid. We are looking more for the Giver than for the gift. And with these outrageous blessings, we will find him within our hearts.

> *"So if you who are evil know how to give good gifts to your children, all the more will your Father in Heaven give good things to those who ask him!" (Mt 7:11)*

And you

Listen as you pray today. Avoid bargain hunting: "You do this for me and I'll do that for you." We do not get good grace cheap; it is always free. And it comes at the Giver's discretion. Because God is God, he knows what we need, what is best for us. Let our thank yous always end with, *Gratefully Yours.*

7

Pass the Torch

Prayer

Whenever we go camping, someone has to take charge of the fire. Everyone can help build it by collecting stones for the circle and sticks for fuel, but someone takes responsibility for the campfire. Is it well-built? Is it safe and secure? Do we have enough kindling and fuel? Who wants to find the fire fizzling on a cold afternoon as the sun sets? Without hesitation we stoke the fire until it rekindles. So it is with the fire of fervor, which gives light and warmth to our life of faith.

This light was lit at the baptismal font. After years as adults we might realize that our baptismal garment needs a few cycles in the wash with the bleach of sorrow and the starch of grace. We have the duty to pass on not just belief in the truths of faith, but also the importance of prayer. If we have children, they need to see us pray, but they also need to *hear* us pray.

Of course, even parents—perhaps especially parents—need private prayer times. So many concerns and preoccupations are involved in raising a family, in *being* family. However, many opportunities arise to pray out loud as a family, for example, saying a prayer before and after meals and to attend Sunday Mass. If we take this glorious duty seriously as a family—being on time, attentive, responsive—imagine the effect on the kids. You may also have the custom of saying the rosary or night prayers together. Some people have the practice of offering short prayers such as, "I guess that means we need to say a little prayer," or "God bless that poor man!" Others generously give sincere blessings to everyone. Do not be shy about speaking with and about God in the presence of others. Offering this glimpse into your relationship with the Lord will be one of the most lasting treasures you can leave to your young ones.

> *One generation shall extol your achievements to another,*
> *and they shall declare the accomplishments of your might.*
> *(Ps 145:4)*

And you

Reflect on how you learned to pray—not just by saying the words of favorite prayers, but by actually conversing with God as with a trusted Friend. Ask him now to give you the courage and skill to convey this relationship to another. Realize that this is best done by *doing* it.

~~~~~~ *8* ~~~~~~~~~~~~~~~~~~~~~~~~~~~~~~~

Praying the Hours

Prayer

What would life be without clocks? They are everywhere: on walls, dashboards, phones, computers, wrists. Our favorite, of course, is the alarm clock perched next to the bed, waiting anxiously to startle us into a new day. Once upright beside our bed, we shuffle off to prepare ourselves to meet the challenges of the next twenty-four hours. Mercifully, most of us have strings of pretty identical days. They require very little innovation, so we can save our mental muscles and sail through the tasks at hand. Despite the grudge you probably hold against your alarm clock, you have glanced at your various clocks a number of times before backing out of the garage. What do you really do with all that time? If you can get all your daily ducks in a row, you might consider *doing the hours*. Actually, I am not referring to the Church's official prayer, the Office or Liturgy of the Hours. I am thinking of the practice of blessing the hours of the day. You may not be able to concentrate on each of the twenty-four, but when it occurs to you that the hour has changed, offer a little prayer: "Thank you, God, for a rockin' ten," or "My praise for a lovely eleven!" Each hour brings us some blessing. It might be a moment of joy and laughter with a friend, a chance to share a family meal, or an opportunity to practice a needed virtue. And beyond this, each one of them has brought us deeper into the gift of life, holding out the graces prepared just for us by our loving God. Each tick of time marks a heartbeat, a step closer to our blessed destiny. What, then, is not to like about a new day?

I will bless the LORD at all times; his praise is constantly on my lips. (Ps 34:2)

And you

Some of us find time a torment, the big bad trickster out to trip up our day. Others thrive on marching minutes into hours with perfect order and purpose. Most people, however, use time to accomplish their daily deeds as competently as possible. The nice thing about time is that it is there to be lived, so, however you face the time at your disposal, you can draw it into your plan of prayer.

9

Fighting Words

Prayer

Life is no picnic. Something always urgently needs attention. If we expect that life as a believer will get easier and prayer will become more routine, this isn't the religion for us — although I can't imagine that any religion promises a bed of roses in this life. The roses are there, but so are the thorns. Healthy bushes require work—mulch, manure, pruning, and praise. Good gardening is down and dirty stuff. So is our life of discipleship.

The *Catechism of the Catholic Church* speaks of "the battle of prayer" (no. 2725). Because we constantly fight inner and outer conflicts, we have to expect to struggle in our prayer life too. Just as the pursuit of virtue and integrity is ongoing, so is the attempt to pray sincerely. We are speaking of a whole person here; it is all *me*: life and prayer, one struggle. If things appear to even out, we most likely aren't being attentive. Our prayer, no matter how sweet and consoling it may be at times, consists of fighting words. We may find ourselves talking tough to God: "You *must . . .*" "For goodness' sake, *where are you?*" "*When are you going to get involved here?*" "Do something *now!*"

And, I dare say, God likes to hear us speak this way. He knows we are fighting for his cause, for the good. These words show that we are serious and engaged in the battle. We own the fight!

> *At the same time God bore witness through signs and wonders and all sorts of mighty deeds, and by distributing the gifts of the Holy Spirit according to His will. (Heb 2:4)*

And you

Now is the time to recall your Confirmation and the graces it promised to put at your disposal. This sacrament made you a witness of our faith, obliged to defend and spread it. This requires speaking up and sharing beliefs and convictions. In fact, your soul was marked forever as an adult disciple. The Holy Spirit takes up residence within us as within a fortified position, confident that we will stand up as Christians proud and true.

10

Individually Wrapped

Prayer

Have you ever opened the company Christmas gift to find funky socks emblazoned with the firm's logo and, of course, "one size fits all"? Well, this isn't how we receive the gift of prayer. Yes, prayer is a gift—it is an expression of the grace within us (grace also being a gift). Since we do not have to manufacture grace or prayer, we sometimes only see it as a pre-packaged religious commodity. We open prayer books as if they were instruction manuals, expecting a voilà experi ence. That, however, would make prayer a magic trick, which it certainly isn't. We all witness to this fact every time we fail to receive what we have prayed for. Prayer is more like the gift of skin that grows with us and surrounds us, holds us together and makes us beautiful. We are each individually wrapped in prayer. None of us prays exactly as any other. Just think of the differences in our ways of speaking, so many nuances, so many subtle or strident characteristics. Basically, prayer is the Holy Spirit speaking in and through our spirit, so it will be all of our peculiarities painted holy. In prayer we offer up expressions of God's concern and love in our own words. The gift of prayer enables us to make a unique contribution.

> *In him you have been enriched in every way, in speech and in knowledge, for our testimony about Christ has become established in you to such an extent that there is no grace you lack, as you await the revelation of our Lord Jesus Christ who will sustain you until the end, so that you'll be blameless on the day of our Lord Jesus Christ. (1 Cor 1:5–8)*

And you

Think of everything that is particularly *you*. What characteristics distinguish you even among members of your family? Are you comfortable with these unique things? How does this self-awareness enter into your prayer? Take some moments to imagine what God intends for you as one so individually wrapped in his grace. Spend a few more moments planning how you will show your gratitude to God and how you want to share your particular gifts with others.

In Praise of Praise

Prayer

In my humble opinion, some of today's cupcakes should be constructed upside down so that the cake itself has a fighting chance for attention. Frosting is necessary, but we are talking cup*cakes* here! If I were a cupcake queen, I would make my frosting in the less sweet European style and use it only as a tasteful accent.

This modern frosting phenomenon does make me think of the one form of prayer that can never be overdone: the prayer of praise, or adoration. We can never pile it on too high! God deserves superlatives. However, since God is God, even our paltry efforts please him. By this I mean the times when the mind gets tongue-tied as it realizes what the heart intends to say.

This also happens in the presence of our idols (if you will excuse the use of that term here): movie stars, sports heroes, and other public figures. We have prepared our words of glowing praise and then find ourselves standing speechless before them. So to be without words before God is to be expected. Like Moses at the burning bush (see Ex 3), we remove our sandals; we put aside our worldly concerns and feel the awe. At times like this we can simply rely on our positive vibes. They will find their way to the presence of God. When you visit the Blessed Sacrament at church, or pay a simple visit to God dwelling within you in a moment of quiet prayer, be lavish in praise. If you find it difficult, begin small with the oft-repeated prayer of praise: *Glory be to the Father, to the Son, and to the Holy Spirit, as it was in the beginning, is now, and ever shall be, world without end. Amen.* Remember that in praise the only way is up!

> *Praise the LORD—it is so good. Sing psalms to our God—it is so sweet. Praise is fitting. (Ps 147:1)*

And you

One of the best-known forms of praise is a list of blessings called the Divine Praises, usually prayed at Exposition of the Blessed Sacrament. You can make up your own litany of praise, basing it on the ways God has been present to you. Be inspired by thoughts of beauty, truth, and goodness, which together are an apt definition of God's wonderfulness. Simply let out all the stops!

12

Spitefully Yours

Prayer

When I was brand new in religious life and rather unfinished, I got very upset over something. Now I can't even remember what it was. I was offended, however, and said to myself, "I'll show *them*. I'm going to just walk out. Then *they* will be sorry." But the moment the last phrase left my mouth, I realized that *I* was the one who would really be sorry. The loss would definitely be mine. Lesson learned!

There is no prayer of spite (thank goodness). Spite is actually the back side of appreciation, and it is a vice. We can think of vice as the tail side of a coin, while virtue is the head. Both are sides of the same coin, just opposites. So, if we feel spite or jealousy, or if we are vengeful or hateful, we need to flip the coin. Flip, if you can, to the opposite feeling. Sometimes this attempt at reversing course may be clumsy and feel insincere, but the more often we try, the more often we will succeed. Of course, we might have a perfectly just reason for feeling as we do, but it is only a natural feeling. As disciples of Christ, we must lay claim to the virtue that is ours by right through our baptismal adoption. Now, as a son or daughter of God, a brother or sister of Jesus Christ, we claim the powerful assistance of the Holy Spirit to convert the currency of sin into virtue. All we have to do is ask!

> *Put off the old man, your former way of life which is corrupted by deceitful desires! Be renewed in your mind and spirit and put on the new man created in accordance with God's design in true righteousness and holiness. (Eph 4:22–24)*

And you

Think of something that usually sets you off. How does this reaction affect you? Don't think about the cause or a possible perpetrator, but concentrate only on how you would rather react when upset. Pray for that!

~~~~~~~~ *13* ~~~~~~

Praying Windows

Prayer

Our souls are meant to be like stained glass windows, so beautiful when bright sunlight streams through them. After dark their beauty can still be seen because of the inner light.

Have you ever reflected on the *soul* of the actual stained glass windows in your church? They were created to depict specific religious scenes special to your parish. Imagine how these windows have affected people through the years. Now they wait for your attentive gaze.

I suggest the practice of *making the windows,* just as we make the Stations of the Cross. Give a few moments to each window (or divide them over several visits), study the image, and say a little prayer. If the windows are symbolic or simply glorious swashes of color, then prayer may take some imagination. But amazing prayers can arise from beauty. Perhaps some windows depict our Lord in one or another of his mysteries, or Mary under one of her titles, or saints favored by the founding members of the parish. Ask the intercession of these saints for the parish, for your family, or for your personal needs. Among them you may find Saint Anne, patron of mothers and grandmothers; Saint Peter, the patron of Christian disciples, bishops, and doubters; or Saint Joseph, patron of husbands, fathers, adoptive and foster parents, workers, good death, and so much more. If donors of the windows are named on the glass, you could also pray for them and their descendants (and the present saints within your parish).

Compose a litany of your window saints with specific intentions in mind, for example, *Saint Thomas More, patron of lawyers and politicians, pray for us.* The saints were just as human as we are today; they lived in different times, but they had needs, problems, and prayers surprisingly like our own. As you admire the light streaming through their images, realize that the same light comes through you.

> *Those who are wise shall shine like the brightness of the sky, and those who lead many to righteousness, like the stars forever and ever. (Dan 12:3)*

And you

You may not consider yourself a saint, but technically speaking, you are. The gift of baptism makes you one. Like the statues that adorn our churches, however, we do have to keep ourselves well-dusted. Ask yourself how you strive to keep the light of grace shining in your life. Speak to our Lord about this daily.

14

Group Hug

Prayer

Some time ago I had the opportunity to visit our Sisters in our convent in Hawaii. The first evening was so lovely that we decided to sit on the beach for night prayer. A free sunset would be included. No sooner were we situated, recollected, and ready, when the sand cleaning tractors arrived, working very slowly and meticulously. Well, we had to scramble to a higher spot, and the noise made shared prayer impossible.

Life offers many times for togetherness: class reunions, office parties, and family gatherings. Amid the flashing cameras someone always yells out, "Group hug!" Reactions range from the one who clings to others like cat hair on an electric night to the more formal hand-shaker.

Our faith also invites us to gather. Although we do gather to celebrate Eucharist and other special occasions, a growing number of people feel a longing to meet simply for prayer together. In these prayer groups the key is to keep the gathering small and intimate. What happens? Usually group prayer centers on a sharing of God's word—nothing scholarly, just individual reflections. A Scripture passage is usually chosen from the readings in the Sunday liturgy. After the text is read aloud once or twice, a time for private reflection follows. Then each person states the words or phrase that most impressed them. Next, each one is invited to share some short reflection on the reading. Usually participants will find a connection to everyday life or some current concern. Spontaneous prayers are offered.

In this shared prayer, called *Lectio Divina* or Divine Reading, we witness the very real presence of the Holy Spirit at work among the disciples of Christ. Amazing unplanned insights arise; prayers are spoken from the unsuspected hidden riches of souls. Often other initiatives result from these sharings. However, the richest result is growth in the understanding of ourselves as one body in Christ, part of a great eternal group hug.

> *"For where two or three are gathered in my name, I am there among them." (Mt 18:20)*

And you

You may have the habit of sharing prayer with family or friends. If not, look for "likely suspects" to propose forming a prayer group. Begin modestly, with few expectations and no specific rules. The object is sharing, openness to the Spirit, and prayer. The reward will be a deeper embrace of faith.

15

The Rosary River

Prayer

Whenever I visit an art museum I find myself magnetically attracted to water scenes. I am fascinated (and frightened) by the reckless abandon of great ships at sea, and delighted by waterfalls of any size. How magical that an artist can render waves and foam, spray and splash so realistically! My favorites, however, are the brooks and rivulets that wend through the pastoral scenes of the great masters. The soothing sensation invites my soul to roam freely through reflections.

Similar calmness results from the restful recitation of the rosary. The rosary is a many-splendid prayer, which can be prayed in so many ways. It can be said as a straight recitation. Usually this is how we pray it while doing something that requires most of our attention, for example when driving. With the luxury of time, we can truly meditate on the rosary. This can be done in various ways. One way is to reflect at length on the particular event of each mystery, for example, the Baptism of Jesus, or the Crowning with Thorns, followed by the appropriate prayers. Some people find it helpful to have a short thought before each Hail Mary. My favorite way is to focus entirely on the meditation of the particular mystery as the prayers flow automatically in the background, like a gentle river of prayer.

However one prefers to pray this important Marian prayer, we keep in mind that the rosary is also a "Gospel Prayer." As we travel spiritually through the events of our Lord's life in the New Testament accounts, we are accompanied by Mary, his Mother and our own. She will point out what is most beneficial to us personally and whisper words for our dialogue with her Son.

They all devoted themselves single-mindedly to prayer, along with some women and Mary the mother of Jesus and his brothers. (Acts 1:14)

And you

Take a good look at your daily schedule. Try to set aside fifteen or twenty minutes (or longer) to sit with Mary and reflect on the mysteries of our salvation—mysteries that began one day as she quietly prayed. If other obligations already claim your time, determine to pray at least one of the twenty rosary mysteries daily. It will be like having a consoling phone conversation with your Mother. Discuss with her the mysteries of your life.

 **16**

XXOOXO

Prayer

Some folks seem unable to express feelings in words. Others make their feelings known through symbols. They hire a blimp to float by with the declaration of undying love that they couldn't speak. Over the years countless apples have appeared on the desks of teachers. At ball games we join the stadium wave since players can't hear our encouragement from up in the ten-thousandth row. These are all symbolic gestures. Sometimes we assemble as a crowd to show support for a cause. We offer shy smiles of gratitude to strangers or place a flag on our lapel in silent tribute to a local hero. These are all visual signs of what we hold deep in our hearts. They could be spoken aloud, but the outward sign is enough.

While symbols are legitimate forms of communication—evidenced by our electronic world—they aren't always enough. It's wonderful to open a message and find a string of Xs and Os, but when the giver is present we want real hugs and kisses. It's the same with God. How dear all of our efforts are to him, but he must love to hear our voice and see our face and feel our participation in the prayer and worship of the Church, the family of believers.

Sometimes we're reluctant to come to church; our sudden appearance may cause some structural damage. "The roof will fall in," we say. Maybe we're exaggerating or a bit embarrassed for staying away. Necessities and emergencies may arise: God understands this. However, he's holding out hope that this week we'll all come.

> Sing a new song to the LORD, sing his praise in the congregation of the faithful believers. (Ps 149:1)

And you

If you're a person who feels you express prayer better among the beauties of nature and the quiet of your own heart, allow me to challenge you. What you speak in the inner room of your heart is really essential, but God also deserves celebration. It is hard to hold a one-man party. Celebration cries out for participation. And while it's true we can pray anywhere, we can only receive the Eucharist at Mass. The Eucharistic Celebration is a family affair where we celebrate the redeeming love of God. And the Church community is a good place to express this because, although we're one voice among many, God can pick us out among all the others.

17

The Old Ticker

Prayer

For my twenty-first birthday my grandmother sent me a laminated prayer card entitled "Growing Old Gracefully." At the time I attributed it to her delightful sense of humor. She regularly typed up pages of jokes "to lighten my days in the convent." Now, as I reread the card, I realize this was really my grandmother's wisdom speaking.

I should have memorized that card or carried a copy in my pocket all these years. Take a look at this: *Keep me from the fatal habit of thinking I must say something on every subject and on every occasion,* or, *Make me thoughtful but not moody, helpful but not bossy.* The prayer also asks for freedom from the need to recite a litany of personal ills and for the ability to admit that occasionally I might remember stories incorrectly. Finally, it asks for the grace of reasonable sweetness and the ability to see and acknowledge good even in the unexpected.

I, for one, am in danger of becoming a living bumper-sticker: *We get too soon old and too late smart.* But luckily I have plenty of time left as long as I have even a little time. It is never too late to pray for wisdom and for all those little virtues that make a person a pleasant companion. This, of course, goes also for young folks—remember I've had the prayer card since I was twenty-one.

So what is the most recommended virtue to start praying for? I think they're really twins: awareness and humility. Ask the Master of life for awareness of your actions and attitudes, and the ability to admit that this or that word or act wasn't the best you could have done. If the occasion warrants it, an apology will go a long way to soothe hurt feelings and clarify your own conscience.

> *So teach us to keep account of our days that we may gain a wise heart. (Ps 90:12)*

And you

Despite life being a long road to travel, the fact is *tempus fugit*! Time truly flies! Whatever time consists of, it passes quickly, so wisdom tells us to spend it as well as we can. Take some of that time right now to reflect on the virtues you have tried to build into your everyday life, and how you deal with your inevitable failures. Pray for awareness and humility.

The Last Roundup

Prayer

As kids we had our favorite cowboy heroes. Sitting tall in the saddle under an oversized ten-gallon hat, he was the best shot and could spin a lasso with extraordinary skill. He was cleverer, quicker, keener, and certainly more just than anyone else for miles around. Whether or not he wore the big silver star, he was definitely the good guy. His many heroic adventures most likely included an exciting cattle roundup where our hero had to outwit and outride the rustlers. My friends and I spent weekends galloping around the backyard on our imaginary horses, righting every wrong while herding and branding unseen longhorns.

As adults in the very real world, a great last roundup awaits us. Jesus himself has described it in the Gospel (cf. Mt 25:31–46). At the end of the world, we will be summoned to this roundup, and called to an account of our Baptism. Matthew's picture may not be as exciting an image as stamping and snorting cattle. His account of the Last Judgment depicts us as sheep and goats (and for story value: the sheep are good and the goats bad). Jesus, the Divine Judge, will have the angels separate the multitude before his throne into two distinct groups: he will pull out his list with all those kindnesses we could've, should've, would've done if we were really riding high in our saddles. Let's face it, though, sometimes we slipped up. At times we rode with the wrong crowd or just wandered off alone.

The good news for us is that we haven't been rounded up yet. We still have plenty of time to right the wrong in our own lives. To do this, our best weapon is prayer.

So then each of us will render an account of ourselves to God. (Rm 14:12)

And you

Go to the Gospel and read the account of the Last Roundup (Judgment). Pay attention to how Jesus says he will evaluate us: not as cattle are judged by size or sleekness, but by our activated prayer, that is, by how our beliefs affected our actions, but especially by our love and compassion. By your interaction with others would anyone suspect you are Christian?

19

Celebrity Facts

Prayer

As we wait in almost any checkout line dozens of smiling, sad, exuberant, and exhausted faces stare at us. We are surrounded. In fact, it is difficult to find a place to gaze where all those eyes aren't watching us. Worse yet, even in the dead of winter, when we have to trudge through snow up to our ears, wearing five or six layers of bulky clothes, these staring-ones keep on flaunting their perfect beach bodies. Yes, of course, these perfect folks are just photos on various celebrity magazines. And even if you don't add a copy to your purchases, you will come home and open your computer or flick on the television only to find those same celebs, in those same poses, with those same faces right there in front of you. As annoying as it may appear, the perfect lives of these perfect people fascinate many of us. We read the rags; we follow the stories; we remember the facts of who is now with whom, and who is doing what where. But why? Is it merely curiosity, or do we envy them? In our more sane moments we realize those fabricated lives are often hollow and sometimes even discombobulated. Do we seriously wish we were them, living their lives?

We have a perfect life to live and an admirable way to follow. We can freely buy into the celebrity of Jesus Christ. It is possible to follow his exploits and read his every word in the Gospels. And he makes himself available for interviews day and night. We can speak to Jesus whenever we want, about anything at all. More than that, he wants to be part of our humble, little lives. He follows our daily activities no matter how insignificant they are. He is moved by all of our expressions because he knows their cause.

> *All the people were overcome with wonder and kept saying to one another, "What sort of word is this?" . . . And news of him went out to every place in the surrounding region. (Lk 4:36–37)*

And you

Take advantage of your personal relationship with Jesus. He is certainly the most fascinating Man. Think of how much he knows about you and how close he wants to be to you. Speak up and talk to him about your feelings.

20

The Man of the House

Prayer

Mary and Jesus depended on him: Joseph, the man of the house of Nazareth. We never hear his voice in the Gospel, yet everything depended on him. It started with his parents who raised him to be a reliable worker, a man of principle who had a gentle disposition and strong faith. When the scandal of an unexpected pregnancy threatened his relationship with Mary, Joseph reviewed his options and prayed. As he slept, God sent a messenger in a dream to Joseph to reassure him about taking Mary as his wife; that her child was of God; and that he, Joseph, would be the boy's "father." From that moment Joseph became husband, father, and man of the house. He was a heroic figure of Scripture and certainly so in the eyes of Mary and Jesus who daily felt his care, protection, example, and love. He provided for his little family, saved them from dangers, led them in prayer, guided them in pilgrimage to Jerusalem. He taught Jesus his trade, raised him in their religious traditions, and modeled for him manly virtues.

What would the story of our salvation have been without this man? Perhaps God would have found someone else to raise his Son, but what a great loss that would have been to Christianity. This quiet man is more than a role model for Jesus and loving spouse to Mary; he is the perfect example for us as well. We have Mary, of course, but she is the Virgin Mother, whereas Joseph is a "real person." He is so normal that without his involvement with Jesus and Mary, we would never have heard of him. He is the perfect example for us because he lived his life in integrity, adapting himself to events without losing his focus. He was straight and true, the just man, that is, he was right with God and man.

" . . . A man after my own heart, one who will do all my will." (Acts 13:22)

And you

Ordinarily it isn't a good idea to compare ourselves to others, but when it comes to Saint Joseph it is an excellent idea. We pray to him not just to sell a house, but to make a home.

He had to work hard to earn a living and guide his family through good times and bad. Look at the events in the Gospels that speak of him (see Mt 1–2; Lk 1–2). Imagine what he must have prayed at those times.

Postured Prayer

Prayer

The first time I saw a praying mantis I was mesmerized because it really appeared to be praying. But it was no more attentive than our childhood teddy bears that knelt next to us as we said our night prayers. Although the bear said nothing, God got some extra love simply by our imagining that the stuffed toy was praying.

Does posture really matter in prayer? Does God care if we are sitting, standing, or kneeling? Or lying down for that matter? It probably doesn't make much difference to God.

Years ago I saw a movie about Saint Ignatius of Loyola. He challenged a nobleman named Beltran to a game of chess. The loser would do the will of the winner for a whole month. Yes, Ignatius won, and Beltran had to spend the month reading and reflecting on *The Spiritual Exercises* (written by Ignatius). And, yes, Beltran saw the folly of his ways and was converted. But what impressed me was the sight of Beltran lying on his bed meditating. I could do that, I thought. If it worked so well for him, imagine what it could do for me.

Although our prayer posture most probably doesn't concern God, it is very important for us. Posture indicates our attitude toward what we are doing. Most likely we wouldn't plop ourselves down and throw one leg over the arm of a chair in the presence of the pope or the president. Our good sense would tell us that they deserve respect. Likewise, when we are praying, especially in public but also in private, we place ourselves in a posture worthy of what we are doing, a posture that says we know this is important, a posture that indicates respect for God and for self. Nevertheless, since we try to keep available to prayer at all times, we will pray in odd and assorted postures during our day. Certainly the principal concern is to be reverent, which is the posture of the soul.

Pray at all times in the Spirit with every manner of prayer and supplication. (Eph 6:18)

And you

Regardless of whether you pray better sitting or kneeling, practice posture of the heart. And try to take a physical stance that expresses your attitude of prayer, that is, to praise, to implore, to adore, to beg mercy.

22

Make Me Better

Prayer

Being sick is no fun. How many times in life have we found ourselves saying: *Make me better!* Our first and best physician was most often Dr. Mom. She seemed to have a magic cure for just about any ailment, from mumps to mosquito bites. She was so proficient that often she could cure with a mere kiss.

As we grow older, we make acquaintance with more serious illnesses and injuries that require frequent visits to doctors, and in turn lead to treatments, hospital stays, medical leaves, incapacities, long recoveries, early retirement, and countless medications. Finding oneself in this state can dishearten those who still have many responsibilities in life, such as parents of young children, or persons who are caring for elderly parents. Energies wane to a low ebb and virtues can be sorely tried.

When we are ill we look for compassion and assistance, but especially prayer. We find that we request prayer from just about everyone. But how do we pray for ourselves?

Certainly we seek out Jesus, the Divine Physician, and perhaps Our Lady of Lourdes, Saint Joseph, Saint Peregrine, Saint John Paul II, or some other favorite intercessor. But we should ask: What do *I* pray for? Of course, we ask that our health be restored, or that we can accept our condition, or, if the illness is terminal, that we will have a holy death. But shouldn't we also pray: *Make me better!*

"Lord, let me learn from this suffering to see the preciousness of life, of *my* life. Let me see more clearly your plan for me here and hereafter. Make me better. Through this illness make me a better person. Make me more like you, Lord."

"Jesus is the one who made me healthy." (Jn 5:15)

And you

Jesus is the one who makes us healthy, although not always with a cure. Replay in your mind the times you profited from an illness or misfortune. How has suffering, no matter how slight it may have seemed, made you a better person? How has it given you more confidence in prayer?

23

In Too Deep

Prayer

Water can be a terrifying thing. Going down with a ship probably ranks high on many people's nightmare list. It happened to me once. Actually, I went down without a ship. I went to the community pool with the neighbors, stepped in, and promptly sank to the bottom. There I stood interminably, or so it seemed. Thanks be to God, panic finally kicked in where good sense didn't, and I pushed off for the surface. I have hated swimming ever since.

I was a little girl then, probably about eight. I'd like to think that my panic included at least a touch of prayer, but I don't remember if it did.

This same kind of thing happened to Saint Peter as a grown man. Jesus had sent the whole crew of disciples off by boat to Gennesaret. Looking across the lake at some point, Jesus saw them battling strong waves, rowing hard, but making little headway. He went to assist them.

The disciples saw a figure walking toward them on the surface of the roiling water. It was dark. They were tired and unnerved by the danger of the storm, and now this sight terrified them. But Jesus called out, identifying himself. Immediately, Peter forgot the trouble they were in and said, "Lord, if it's you, command me to come to you on the water." "Come," Jesus said. Peter jumped from the boat and found that he, too, could walk on the water. Suddenly, realizing what *he* was doing, Peter's faith faltered and he sank into the waves.

From time to time we get caught up in panic mode. This can even occur in prayer. Usually it follows an unexpected perception. "I am in a dangerous situation and can't see my way out." "This illness is life-threatening, but I'm not ready to die." "God really spoke within me and now I'll have to change my life." The only thing we need to do at these moments is to reach out to God in prayer.

"Save me, Lord!" (Mt 14:30)

And you

How do you face the large or small spiritual panics of life? Do you fight the troubling waters or attempt to swim to unseen safety? Do you try to climb out of the problem or call to friends for help? Or do you immediately cry out like Peter, "Save me, Lord"?

~~~~~ *24* ~~~~~~~~~~~~~~~~~~~~~~~~~~~~~~~~~~

Psalm Your Heart Out

Prayer

Sometimes in the middle of a novel or a movie it suddenly hits me: yes, that is exactly how I feel, too. A good piece of writing can prompt one of those *aha* moments.

It is all too true that we can come to prayer with our soul frozen shut. Prayer sometimes needs a prompt, too. This is one of the blessings of the Psalms. They are 150 cheat sheets for prayer. These wonderful prayers can crack open the heart. Sometimes a book of the Psalms or a larger Bible will provide a table suggesting which psalm is more appropriate for what need. *Yes, I really would like to say or do that, but since I cannot, let me at least pray it.* The Psalms exult, and they also disparage; they plead and prod. They are the all-purpose prayer guide. They address all the seasons of the heart, as well as some in-between seasons we never imagined.

As the ultimate text book on prayer, the Psalms delve deeply into human joy and sorrow, perplexity and pain. The Psalms model for us true, heartfelt, life-saturated prayer.

As with all other printed prayers, the Psalms are to be interpreted by the pray-er. For example, we do not want our enemies to die by the sword, but we might want them to die to sin by being pierced through by the power of God's word. While most city dwellers cannot find a green pasture to lie down in, we can certainly find rest in the refreshing mercy of God.

Psalming is the prayer of the heart. In prayer our feelings often hold sway over the reason and will. And this is good because most prayers are filtered through the heart.

For this my soul will no longer keep silent but sing psalms to you. (Ps 30:12)

And you

Just like our feelings, our prayer can be held close to the vest or worn on our sleeve. Do you know where your prayer resides? Try expressing what you feel by making up your own personal psalms. You might include some familiar symbols in your prayers, for example, your favorite sport, your kitchen implements, your work processes, the plants in your garden. Remember, this is you praying your feelings in your world.

Hope of Heaven

Prayer

This is our hope: to reach heaven. We profess our belief in the Creed: I believe . . . in life everlasting. But what is heaven? Anyone with a clear idea, please raise your hand!

It is very difficult to formulate a good picture of heaven. We were created for heaven; we want it; we anticipate it, but what is heaven? We find little consolation in the great Apostle Paul who, although taken up into heaven, could not describe it. He only said, "Eye has not seen, nor ear heard what is in store for us there, nor is it possible to explain" (cf. 2 Cor 12:4).

We do have one very reliable witness in Jesus himself. In his Sermon on the Mount (see Mt 5:1–12) he offers us a window into heaven. For example he says, "Blessed are the poor in spirit, for theirs is the Kingdom of Heaven. Blessed are the pure of heart, for they shall see God." To me, this latter one says it all: they (we) shall *see* God. Heaven is being with God, being in his presence forever. What will we do in heaven? Despite our happy speculation, no one really knows. It will likely not be all harps and haloes, however.

Great artists usually depict the saints in heaven as standing before the throne of God, basking in the splendor of the Almighty. At first blush that may not sound too exciting, but on reflection it should be enough to sustain us now. For me, being happy forever is a pretty appealing proposition. The next question is this: How do we prepare for eternal happiness? Do we pray for it? For this we can return to the Eight Beatitudes. They are a prayer to be lived. Not only are they given to us to read and reflect upon, but also to pray and live.

So we're always full of courage, even though we know that while we're at home in the body we're away from the Lord, for we walk through faith, not by sight. (2 Cor 5:6–7)

And you

Pick up your Bible or go online and read the Beatitudes (Mt 5:1–12). Pray them thoughtfully, perhaps beginning with a few words of gratitude: "Thank you, Jesus, for these beautiful promises." Then ask yourself how the Beatitudes can be seen in your life.

Stepping Out

Prayer

Aside from summer vacations, city dwellers wear shoes. We all started out barefoot, but it didn't take long before our baby feet were fitted into their first shoes. Truthfully, baby shoes aren't necessary. Their *raison d'être* is cuteness.

Most family females delight in shopping for baby clothes, and *cute* is a major factor in what they purchase. Soon, however, *cute* falls in line behind useful, supportive, sturdy, and reasonably priced. Fashionable shoes are just that: a statement of taste. But for walking or exercising, standing all day, and doing various chores, we prefer solid, comfortable footwear.

This is also the story of our prayer. Little ones are taught charming prayers about love and friendship and care. As we grow in age and understanding, we learn sturdy, practical prayer that will hold up amid the hard work and activity of our life. Often these prayers are the ones we say together, aloud. They are called vocal prayers, such as the Our Father, the Hail Mary, the Glory Be, the responses at Mass, the Liturgy of the Hours, parish novenas, the rosary, or even family morning or evening prayers. These are our practical prayers. They are solid, supportive, and comfortable.

There are times, however, for stepping out when we don our dressier prayers. These, like our best shoes, are worn with real purpose. We offer these prayers with the personal touch. They distinguish us among the many who pray. They might sound like this: "Lord, I need some extra attention today." "Yes, today I am here with my best prayer because I want to celebrate your love for me." "Dear God, this is a solemn occasion. I have come to commend my father's soul to your care." "Lord, I've come about a friend."

In fact, whenever we turn to spontaneous prayer we are stepping out in prayer.

> *"Therefore, I tell you, don't worry about your life, what you'll eat, or about the body, what you'll wear; isn't life more than food, and the body more than clothing?" (Mt 6:25)*

And you

How do you feel about praying with others? The prayers we call vocal are our common prayers. Because of them *we* can pray together. Do you think your personal prayer needs more attention? Do you allow your soul to freely fashion prayer? Practice stepping out in prayer according to the moods of your life.

27

Heavy Lifting

Prayer

Christians commonly define prayer as the lifting up of the mind and heart to God. Three words are important: *lifting, mind,* and *heart.* We are directed to engage our whole self in the act of praying: mind, will, and heart—all the faculties of the human spirit. Our mind thinks of God, communicates with him, reflects and meditates on his word. The heart connects with God; it opens to him, embraces him, and pours its love out to him. Meanwhile, the will does the heavy lifting. The will desires and motivates. It is the strong man of the soul. What the mind and heart direct toward God, the will delivers and sustains. We call this energy of the soul our will power.

My father worked for years as a stationary engineer in a plant that produced submarine engines. His responsibility was to keep the boilers running to provide steam 24/7. The plant could never slack off; the energy had to be constantly and consistently available. The demands on our will power are similar. The "boiler" which provides our "steam" is prayer. We need to have a constant and consistent head of steam. If a boiler went out in my father's workplace, disaster ensued. If our will weakens, spiritual disaster can threaten us or, at best, we suffer a setback. What to do? Build up a regimen of prayer. By this, I suggest more regularity than amount; more consistency than severity. Choose devotions that are available to you—those that fit your state in life and your responsibilities. For example, if you have a family, don't bind yourself to an evening novena on the other side of town.

Remember: what goes around comes around. By praying, you provide energy to your will, which in turn powers the intention of your mind and the love of your heart. Then intention and love feed your prayer.

> *For this reason I remind you to stir up the flame of God's gift, which is yours through the laying on of my hands, for God didn't give us a spirit of cowardice—He gave us a spirit of power, love, and good judgment. (2 Tm 1:6)*

And you

Review your prayer power. Do you see yourself well prepared for the heavy lifting of life?

Praying for Success

Prayer

Have you ever prayed for success? Probably we all have. That's good. We should pray about everything we do. We pray for good grades in school, to receive a raise or promotion, even to meet the ideal mate. These are all prayers for success. They are good and even necessary prayers.

In praying for success, do we ever pray as did the mother of the sons of Zebedee? She prayed that her beloved boys would be seated on either side of Jesus in his kingdom. Saint Matthew says that she asked Jesus to *command* that this happen—no wiggle room allowed. She not only wanted job security for them, but also positions of power and prestige. As apostles, both James and John were pillars of the newly formed Church and became great saints. They may have done well on the Lord's right and left, but that wasn't God's plan. Perhaps they were too qualified to assume the position assigned to Peter. Jesus wanted the work of grace, not personal abilities, to be evident in the man who assumed leadership of his flock.

We do need leaders in this life, and many of us are asked to direct the lives of others as parents, teachers, politicians, managers, or many other roles. Jesus makes it abundantly clear that with the position of leadership comes the call to service. In whatever position of responsibility we find ourselves, let us pray to be most successful as servants of the needs of others in imitation of Jesus, who gave "his life as a ransom for many" (Mt 20:28).

"You don't know what you're asking for!" (Mt 20:22)

And you

What is the most urgent thought running continually in your mind? Pin it down and study it for a few minutes. It probably concerns some desire for yourself. Very likely it is for some success.

Now enter your heart and see if you have been praying about this concern. If you realize the prayer aspect is weak, make a mental memo to pray over and about it. Pray about how you will serve others better through the realization of this personal success.

Road Trip

Prayer

Perfect sand, calming sea, the dance and song of a far-off isle—have you felt the lure of an exotic vacation trip? Great numbers of people sign up every year for flights and cruises, treks and climbs. Each trip requires a lot of preparation and expense, as well as paperwork and perhaps even inoculations. Why do so many folks find such trips so compelling? Some yearn to get away and relax. Others thrill at the adventure of discovering something new. Some travelers, however, desire to make a pilgrimage.

What makes a trip a pilgrimage? The first difference between a trip and a pilgrimage is motivation. Although people take many photos on pilgrimages, their purpose is not simply to admire the spot. They undertake a pilgrimage as an act of praise, penance, or petition. People travel to a shrine to offer praise as they celebrate the feast day that shrine commemorates. Sometimes people make a pilgrimage to do penance for a personal or social sin. At other times the intention is to ask for a favor or a particular grace.

All pilgrimages require movement from one place to another, from home to a shrine or a holy place. It could be in another country or a local shrine, perhaps in the next state, town, or parish. A local pilgrimage could be planned in order to attend a Sunday Mass at another parish that is celebrating a feast day special to one of its ethnic communities. Perhaps the traveling statue of Our Lady of Fatima, the Pilgrim Madonna, may be visiting a family nearby.

Pilgrimages have another very important purpose: to remind us that we are each on an individual earthly pilgrimage that will culminate at the ultimate shrine of heaven. Every day we endure the difficulties and admire the beauties along our way, and as we engage with our fellow travelers, it is important to make this pilgrimage prayerfully.

> *I rejoiced when they said to me: "We will go to the house of the LORD." (Ps 122:1)*

And you

If you are housebound or if bad weather arises on the day you have chosen for your pilgrimage, change plans and make a domestic pilgrimage. This can be done by watching a DVD about a shrine or simply by walking from one to another of the sacred images in your home. As you pause before each one, say some special prayers or even a decade of the rosary.

For the Love of (Saint) Mike!

Prayer

Horror and sci-fi rank high among popular film genres. Their story lines allow for the most fantastic scenarios "peopled" by an array of wildly outlandish creatures. Amazingly the audiences include lovers, eleven-year-olds, and level-headed old ladies. Rhyme or reason? Maybe, maybe not. These films appeal to our imagination. Who doesn't like to conjure up "what-ifs"? And isn't there great fun in a good fright?

Strangely, however, it is also true that many people will not hear of hell or the devil. These folks simply will not countenance any serious talk of the reality of evil. Why is this? Responses range from: "those are fairy tales" to "it is too upsetting." Perhaps the reason is that the prospect of evil being a reality is terrifying. I have noticed that when the media portray evil in a more realistic and strident way, the more vehemently do some deny the possibility of evil. To me that in itself is proof of the existence of an intelligent evil spirit.

In all of this, fear should be a factor. When God inspired the biblical writers, he did so as any good filmmaker might. In the very beginning he depicted the epic struggle of good and evil when one of his best "characters," Lucifer, went rogue. When Lucifer, the Light-bearer, led an uprising of like-minded angels in revolt, he was overcome by an equally magnificent and mighty angel appropriately named Who-Is-Like-God, or Michael.

Angelic beings are beyond our understanding but not our imagination, which is why God put them in many strategic places throughout salvation history. Saint Michael is one of the Archangels, a captain, if you will, in God's great spirit world. The angels represent the grand antidote to evil. They are God's messengers and soldiers sent to *light, guard, rule, and guide us*, as the prayer to the Guardian Angels says.

> *I am going to send an angel in front of you, to guard you on the way and to bring you to the place that I have prepared. (Ex 23:20)*

And you

Become familiar with the angels. Saint Michael the Archangel is the protector of the Church and patron of policemen and soldiers. He is also the symbol of heavenly strength showing us God's great power. Daily prayer to your Guardian Angel assures you of the company of a dedicated confidant.

――――― *31* ―――――――――――――――――――――――――

Thanks for Nothing!

Prayer

What does it mean when our prayers aren't answered? Does it mean there isn't really a God up there or that I'm so unimportant that God can ignore me? Before you angrily yell out something regrettable, like, *Thanks for nothing,* consider this: you might be concentrating so much on your request that you don't hear the answer. Prayer is, after all, a conversation. None of us likes to attempt a conversation with someone who can't be interrupted. Some folks simply keep talking right through your questions or replies. They wrote a script and they have to deliver it. No amount of empathy, sympathy, or antipathy will sway them. Why? Because they do not hear any voice but their own.

Could this be happening in our prayer when we feel there is no answer? Has God tried to interrupt us, to break through our words with a reply? Are we carrying on a one-sided conversation and calling it "prayer"? And what if God is saying a very simple "no" to our prayer? This is when a familiarity with God becomes so important. Are we familiar enough with God to trust even when the answer seems to be no? It is said that God's ways are not our ways; God's thoughts are not our thoughts. What does that mean? Honestly, we don't know, but if we are secure in our love for God and God's love for us, we can trust that whatever way he is moving in this or that situation, whatever he is thinking, it is the best for us. It is the best also for those we bring to prayer. God is Wisdom, Goodness, and Love, but, above all, God is God.

In God we trust is not just a national slogan printed on our currency or carved on our buildings. It should also be emblazoned on our souls by our prayer.

> *When I called and you answered me,*
> *you gave me courage: in my soul there was strength.*
> *(Ps 138:3)*

And you

Give yourself a little private time to revisit your last disappointment in prayer. Consider what you were asking. What answer were you hoping for? How did you feel when you realized what answer God had given you? Were you able to express to God your disappointment? How has your prayer life been since then? Speak with God about it now.

32

Just Passing Through

Prayer

Every so often someone walks through our consciousness. We are engaged in normal thoughts and activities when suddenly someone comes to mind. Mrs. Tanish did this recently. I was sitting here at my desk when she gracefully entered the room and sweetly addressed her class of exuberant first graders. For a moment I was swept back in time to that brightly colored classroom where every piece of furniture was a mixture of pink and turquoise.

Another recent visitor was "Mr. Peanut," a man I came across one evening. He was sitting on the ground in an empty parking space, drunk as a fish. Perhaps he is still grateful for his rescue. Other times it might be a school friend or neighbor, some public figure or an unfamiliar face from the news. Just passing through, as it were. Do they come summoned by a word, a tone of voice, some movement, or a particular color? While they may just be a natural phenomenon of our brain's activity, they could also have come to beg for prayer or to bestow a blessing. Whatever evoked thought of them, we have an opportunity to show love, gratitude, or forgiveness to our visitor by means of a little prayer.

In our outward daily lives many chance encounters also happen—persons just passing through. Often we hardly notice them. We pay scant attention to them, not taking advantage of the moment to help them or ourselves by what might transpire. These run-ins may be purely coincidental, but that doesn't render them unimportant. Someone needs a reassuring look, a smile, a word of encouragement. These small gestures can have great meaning. If nothing else, they are human interactions in an often impersonal world. And then, of course, we have the gift of prayer, which we as Christians owe to everyone.

> *Don't forget your duty to be hospitable, for some who were hospitable had angels as guests, without knowing it. (Heb 13:3)*

And you

Imagine how much good you can do for others, living and deceased, by your prayers. Take a couple of moments to recall the last one or two persons who crossed your path or who passed through your mind. Ask the Lord to bless them today.

33

Cold Molasses

Prayer

A well-worn expression speaks about being as slow as cold molasses running up a hill. Just picture a glob of cold, gooey molasses trying this move. It's a ridiculous concept. Being of the slower persuasion myself, I have often heard and overheard this epithet. I'd like to think it's due to a genetic oversight. After all, Great-Grandmother Delano said she'd never seen a slower mortal than her own little girl, my granny.

As with molasses, something can be said for consistency. Consistency is the secret ingredient for the whole spiritual life. This brings to mind another well-used saying: one step forward and two steps back. It may involve plenty of movement, but where does it get you?

The serious Christian always moves onward. To say that we are making spiritual progress means we are getting all of our spiritual ducks in order. We are practicing the virtues, living the Beatitudes and the sacraments, performing the works of mercy, and making the most of every opportunity to do good. All of this begins with and depends on how we pray. The secret to beneficial prayer is consistency. Begin with a few prayers prayed well.

Think of progress in prayer as being similar to a child's backpack. Kindergartners aren't expected to hoist on their backs something heavier than themselves. Only as they grow do they take home more work. In the prayer life we first master the essential prayers and practices; for example, we learn the basic Catholic prayers, then the Mass responses, the formula for making a good Confession, and more. Then we branch out to other devotions of our choosing, for example, the novena to the Sacred Heart of Jesus or the Little Office of the Blessed Virgin. Not every devotion will appeal to us. The trick is not to keep piling them on. Remember consistency. Adopt those devotions and prayers most meaningful to you. Perfect them and let them contribute to perfecting you.

Not that I have already achieved this or that I'm already perfect! But I continue to strive in the hope of making it my own, because Christ [Jesus] has made me his own. (Phil 3:12)

And you

Look over your prayer life from childhood until now. How have you progressed? Do your prayers still sound like those of a child? Can you say that your prayer has matured? Do you pray the needs and joys and sorrows of the life you live today?

Hardly or Heartily?

Prayer

This is a Catholic book, so we were bound to get to personal sin sooner or later. For this topic there is no *sooner or later.* Sin is here and now. And once forgiven, it should be forgotten: over and out. We pray ourselves to, through, and toward the Sacrament of Reconciliation, or Confession. Sometimes we have to get out and push ourselves to the confessional or reconciliation room (presented as a room with chairs, one for the priest, one for the penitent, which usually also has the option for staying anonymously behind a screen). The place used for the sacrament is no longer dark and confining, but as light and airy as the sacrament itself. Once in the reconciliation room, we need to pray ourselves through the act of confession. Let's take for granted that we have examined our conscience, at least somewhat, or we wouldn't be there. What did I do that I knew was wrong? Did I do it even if I only suspected it might be wrong? Did I fail to do something I know I should have done? We can't fudge the facts, because God, to whom we are confessing, knows exactly what we did. In letting us accuse ourselves, we learn an important lesson: to be responsible for our actions. In other words we become adults. And so our Act of Contrition should be an act of maturity. The prayer has us say: "O my God, I am heartily sorry for having offended you." Children sometimes understand the prayer to say that we are *hardly* sorry, but, as mature individuals, we can sincerely say that we are sorry with all of our heart, completely. Our prayer is not only that God, through his priest, will raise his hand in absolution, but that he will hold his protecting hand over us to help us never to sin again.

> *Then Jesus said, "Neither do I condemn you. Go your way, and from now on sin no more." (Jn 8:11)*

And you

Confession is to the soul what a tune-up is to a car. Every so often, the wear and tear of life brings us into God's shop of mercy. How do you pray the Sacrament of Reconciliation? Can you feel the grace of forgiveness? Can you sincerely say you are trying, with God's grace, to avoid whatever for you is an occasion of sin? Frequent Confession gives this grace.

35

Hard Little Pew, I Love You!

Prayer

Yes, from time to time we all wish —if they aren't already— that our church pews were padded. Many people suffer assorted symptoms of arthritis with flare-ups of sciatica thrown in for good measure. Puffy pews would be so heavenly. That's when our angelic shoulder pad starts preaching about the benefits of penance and mortification. So we find ourselves taking sides amid the quibbling of the little red smokin' shoulder pad and the lovely white angelic one. Cushions or hard wood, which is better? Do you suppose it matters greatly in the grand scheme of things? God is more interested in *what* we are saying than in how comfortable we are.

Personally, I sit on the edge of the pew in what I like to think of as good posture. Somehow this helps me stay recollected (awake actually). Others do better in a half-kneeling, half-sitting position. Then there are the cushion-cuddlers.

Most pray-ers, however, are so intent on what they have come to do that they simply kneel or sit in a pew without any expectations. Comfort would be welcome, but it is only a vague background thought. They keep the presence of God front and center in their consciousness.

I imagine these normal, devout folks are praying like the tax collector in the story Jesus told of the two men praying in the temple (see Lk 18:9–14). One was a distinguished fellow in his community, and he prayed with a little too much self-importance. "I do this and I do that. Unlike that fellow in the back row, I pay my dues and then some." The tax collector, or, as we know him, the sinner, instead stayed in the back with his head and his heart bowed. "I am a sinner," he admitted. "Have mercy on me, Lord." It doesn't require much imagination to pick out the prayer that pleased God more.

> O Lord, you have searched me and known me. You know
> when I sit down and when I rise up; you discern my thoughts
> from far away. (Ps 139:1–2 NRSV)

And you

Don't be distracted from prayer by worry about whether you should try to get comfortable or settle into the unforgiving wood. God isn't looking, he's listening. The important thing is how you see yourself in relation to God. All that matters in any time or place is the position of the heart. *Comfort my heart, O Lord.*

36

Eternal Rest

Prayer

The most familiar prayer for the deceased is this: *Eternal rest grant to them, O Lord, and let perpetual light shine upon them. May they rest in peace. Amen.*

To some folks the idea of the dead enjoying eternal rest seems a cop out. Is it just a fancy way to say that all activity has ceased for them? Perhaps Saint Augustine can make it more understandable with his most frequently quoted words: "Our hearts are restless, O Lord, until they rest in you" [*The Confessions*, Book 1, Chapter 1]. Restlessness is part of the human condition. When we are bored, we may become restless. When we feel anxious, we become restless. This inner state may even be obvious in our actions and reactions.

To relax our guard and find repose is to sink into a sense of security and peace. As the well-known Easter hymn sings, "The strife is o'er." Being at peace with God is the rest the soul longs for.

The light we ask for the dead is a warmth and clarity. We experience a physical and mental relief when something finally dawns on us and we can say that we *do* understand what had eluded us. In eternity we will at last and literally see the light.

So what better prayer can we make for our deceased than to wish them peace with God? We ask that God, our good Father, envelop them in his secure embrace and give them insight into the mystery that was their life.

Pray for a happy death, or, perhaps better, a blessed death. That is, ask this for all the dying, and for yourself when your hour comes, that death may call when you are reconciled to your passing, at a time when you have a strong and vibrant faith in your final destination. We all want to die with hope in heaven after having lived life well or having sincerely humbled ourselves for our failings.

> *Right now we see indistinctly, as in a mirror, but then we'll see face to face. At present my knowledge is incomplete, but then I'll truly understand, as God understands me. (1 Cor 13:12)*

And you

You may consider taking on a personal devotion to the dying and deceased. When passing a cemetery, a funeral home, or a hospital, pray for those who have died, or who are at the point of death. Your prayers will accompany these souls on their journey into God's eternal rest.

37

Loves Me, Loves Me Not

Prayer

One Sunday I allowed myself the luxury of attending a late morning Mass. As I was about halfway to Church my attention fell on a woman curled up in a blanket on a doorstep. It was bitterly cold and I must confess my first thought was to continue walking down my side of the street. After all, I'd be late for Mass if I stopped. Then, stunned by my own insensitivity, I walked up to her. A closer view revealed that she was clothed only in that blanket and a pair of mismatched shoes. I asked if I could help her with anything, and she requested bus fare to a nearby city. So little to ask! I gave her the money and told her I would return in a few minutes. I went home and got enough money to buy her some warm clothes and a coat so she could go on her way with renewed dignity. Her smile and blessing were all the thanks I needed. Needless to say I didn't make it to church in time and had to rearrange my afternoon plans to attend evening Mass. Who knows if the Lord sent her just for me that day! I had never seen her before nor have I seen her since. Why does God place such people in our path, on the street corners of our life? Perhaps he wants to rattle our safe little comfort zones and show us close-up and personal what he is preaching in the Gospels. Certainly it gives us an opportunity to live out who we profess to be as Christians. Our initial reaction and our consequent action is prayer lived out. This is vital prayer, red-blooded prayer. We find out if we are truly invested in the business of following Jesus Christ.

> *If a brother or sister is in need of clothes and lacks food for the day and one of you says to them, "Go in peace; stay warm and eat well!" what good is it? And so faith by itself is dead, unless it is manifested in works. (Jm 2:15–16)*

And you

Have you ever been in a situation when you had to choose between attending Mass and attending to the needs of a person? Faith has been installed, but is it working? Every day build into your prayer a look at the real needs of someone else.

38

Poetry of Prayer

Prayer

I am blessed to live with a poet. So often in the years I have known her, Sister Mary Paula has suddenly announced: "This is so beautiful so poignant, or so puzzling, let's write a poem!" And she is right, for life is full of moments that call for poetry. We could liken this poetic impetus to the urge so many people have to capture images on their cell phones. No occasion seems too insignificant to be documented. Significance here lies in the eye of the beholder.

Poetry paints a verbal canvas; it captures an image in words. We enjoy so many types of poetry: the informal, the epic, the sonnet, free verse, and endless others, with such diverse meter, rhyme, and cadence. Isn't this true of prayer, too? It is as unique as the one who utters it. Even one who prays can pray in so many formats, with meter to match the moods of the soul—sometimes full of the rhyme of a reasoned prayer, sometimes full of the helter-skelter wildness and wonder of a spirit in love or in pain. We hope to form our spirits to suddenly burst into prayer. Every experience should call upon the heart for expression. The soul of the poet, like that of my dear sister, is a soul at prayer, and it is contagious. I do not write poetry often, but I have learned to recognize it at work within my prayer.

Thank you, Sister Mary Paula, for the encouragement to let my soul run free over the events of each day. Yes, let's write a poem of prayer with our lives.

Speak to each other in psalms, hymns, and spiritual songs; sing praise to the Lord in your hearts. (Eph 5:19)

And you

Carry around a small notebook to jot down your poetry or prayer. I recommend actual paper, not any electronic device. And don't cheat by looking up words while you are reflecting. Just let it roll off the tip of your soul. Sometimes a poem or prayer won't want to be written. In that case, just let it be. Allow it to simmer within until its secrets rise to God like incense.

~~~~~~~ *39* ~~~~~~~~~~~~~~~~~~~~~~~~~~~~~~~~~~~~~~

Mary

Prayer

When we want to see something clearly, such as fine print, we pull out a magnifying glass. At rallies or sporting events we appreciate the giant screen setup that allows us to see beyond our normal range of view. We are happy about the ability to enlarge and clarify what is beyond us.

Mary has a similar role, as she explains it: *My soul, my very being, magnifies the Lord.* Her first assignment from God was to give flesh to the second Person of the Blessed Trinity, to make him man so that we could relate to him and he to us. She accepted all the trials, misunderstandings, deprivations, and demands included in her role as the Mother of the Christ. When, from the cross, Jesus replaced himself with John, the young apostle, and us by association, Mary continued to instruct, guide, and cherish all who belong to her Son.

Her second assignment was to be our mother. This was difficult for one so humble, but Mary never said no to what God asked of her. Throughout her life Mary's mode of operation was to magnify the Lord, to make him shine. While her soul magnified the Lord, her spirit rejoiced in him.

We treat Mary as grown ups treat their mothers. We protect her image, speak proudly of her, do anything for her, and in return we only ask for the warmth of her love, the security of her presence, and the assurance of her intercession.

We recognize how close she is to God every time we address her with the words: Hail, Mary, full of grace, the Lord is with you.

And Mary said,
"My soul gives praise to the Lord,
and my spirit rejoices in God my Savior." (Lk 1:47)

And you

As adults we don't always appreciate the motherliness of our own mothers. *"I wish she wouldn't get so involved in my life. I'm not a kid anymore,"* you might say. *"I can do this, Mom. Don't you remember how old I am?"* But, really, many of us quickly turn to our mothers when we need help or comfort. Isn't this what brings us to the Mother of Jesus? Pay attention the next time you turn to Mary in prayer. What are you looking for? Mary is not for discipline or demands, but for reminders and comfort. You are never too grown-up for Mary. Let her mother you.

Mini-Martyrdom

Prayer

Have you ever sat down and thought about martyrs? They populate the pages of Church history down to our own day. We tend to picture martyrdom melodramatically: the victim standing or lying in a heroic posture, gaze fixed on heaven, which has opened up gloriously as rays of celestial light illuminate the scene. Oh, and I almost forgot the crowd of awestruck onlookers.

In reality, martyrs probably don't feel much by way of glorious triumph. They may have contemplated the triumph of grace in their sacrifice, but at the moment of martyrdom, no matter how long it may be, they feel human emotions: fear, anguish, pain, and abandonment. They tramp through real dirt, mud, and blood. Real people yell at them, threaten them, push them around. The martyrs are tired, hungry, terrified, abused. This is not a movie that will end by ten. It is real, unremitting, and relentless.

How do they put up with it? Their secret is that they made the choice long before. They decided for Christ and it led them to this. As simple as that! Could any of us do it? Actually, we do! We everyday Christians have many mini-martyrdoms, not unto immediate death, but until the good Lord calls us. Look at your life or the life of someone you admire: many times you must stand with Christ despite discomfort, fear, pain, harassment, or even condemnation. No glorious music plays, no heavenly lights shine, no awestruck crowd admires us when we serve the sick, the demented, the angry, the desperate, the lonely or abandoned; when we literally slave to meet obligations or eliminate debts; when we submit to cruel insults, pranks, ill-treatment, or injustice in order to serve a cause, pursue a dream, or simply raise a family. How often is life an occasion of self-offering: free, genuine, loving, Christ-like, life-giving? This is ordinary Christian martyrdom, a long-chosen, deeply-felt witness to faith.

We pray that you will be strengthened with all the power of his glorious might so that your steadfastness and patience will be perfected. (Col 1:11)

And you

A martyr is a *witness*, and true belief is all about witnessing. In our many mini-martyrdoms, we are living our prayer. Spend some time choosing what God has put on your plate. Thank him for accepting your witness, for trusting you to live out your prayer every day.

Whine and Dine

Prayer

We may often find ourselves entertaining guests who are less than perfect. Who is perfect, after all? However, no one wants to be seated next to a complainer for the evening. For example, when you say "accept," they hear "except." Not even being wrong is safe with complainers. They can find something wrong even with wrong.

When we were young, we called them whiners. They were the downers at the dinner table. Sometimes as adults we raise the habit to new heights: more sophisticated and more severe. Whining and complaining are kith and kin. If we do one, we likely do the other. I'm not sure which of the two is first because the whiner never actually says exactly what is so bothersome. At least the complainer puts it out there loud and clear.

How often do the complainers and whiners think in terms of the Ultimate Dining Experience? In heaven signs hang all around that clearly state: "No Whining Allowed!" Imagine how refreshing and freeing: we will have nothing to complain about. No irritations, no accidental insults, no migraines—mourning will be turned into joy. In heaven each of us, even the whiner, will be perfected. Imagine for once everyone will be eager to listen and we will be speechless: no complaints, only compliments.

One thing I wonder about regarding that Eternal Perfect Moment: Will those impaired in this life be different in heaven? Will their heavenly perfection make them unrecognizable to us? I think not, but I am anxious to see what God will call forth from them. And I wonder, too, about the perfection of the perpetual whiner: What beauty would God like to call forth even now?

Lord, open my lips, and my mouth will declare your praise. (Ps 51:17)

And you

If you catch yourself whining, even if it is more of a whimper, stop yourself and try to put words to it. What are you trying to communicate? Practice turning these concerns into prayers. It is always safe to practice with God. He keeps secrets very well. In fact, he will breathe clarity into our confused thoughts. He will give courage to speak a whine in words. He will make us more perfect guests at the table of life.

42

Platinum Prayer

Prayer

Some popular recording artists sell enough albums to "go platinum." These people can touch hearts, nerves, and sensibilities with their well-crafted words and catchy tunes.

This won't happen in prayer. No heavenly wall plaques will honor our well-crafted words or our clever melodies of prayer. But, as Blessed James Alberione, the twentieth-century apostle of the media, has observed, the strings of our heart do need to be well tuned. By caring well for our instrument, that is our heart, we will always be ready to join in the great Christmas song of the angels, "Glory to God and peace on earth to those of good will." In the great chorus of prayer everyone can snag top honors. Even those whose tone is a little off can succeed at prayer. "God hears the cry of the poor"—it is music to his ears. Why? Does he enjoy seeing human misery or find pleasure in waiting for us to reach a desperate stage? No, but God loves sincerity and truth. He wants integrity even in prayer. He wants us to realize that in good times and in bad, he is the center of our lives. If we are among the poor of any type, God wants us to reach out to him, to search for his fatherly hand, to let him grasp us and hold us. If all is well with us, God still wants to hear our cries. Our cries of joy and satisfaction are also music to God's ears when we direct them to him in gratitude. God wants each of us to know our own reality and to willingly come before him as we are. We should be his adoring sons and daughters no matter whether our cries are of joy or sorrow. He hears and is near—in our hearts.

Sing a new song to him; play the harp skillfully amid shouts of triumph. (Ps 33:3)

And you

How well tuned is your heart? Do you know what tune your heart plays to God? Is it a song of praise and gratitude no matter what circumstances surround it? Let the sound of your integrity reach the ears of God. Give him more reason to rejoice in you.

The Big Dig

Prayer

For many years the life of the city of Boston was bound up in a monumental redesign project involving many of its roadways, tunnels, and bridges. The project fell way behind schedule and ballooned way over budget. It was known affectionately as the Big Dig. This project created jobs for many people while weighing in its balance many a corporate or political career. It caused much speculation and not a little off-site betting. It became like a member of the greater-Boston family, invited into every conversation: "How are things going with the dig over your way?" "Do you suppose it will really wrap up by the holiday?" The only thing that everyone knew was that a whole lot of digging was going on.

The Big Dig was a source of inconvenience over the years and was plagued by many problems. Now completed, it serves the city well. It has re-routed traffic and indirectly helped to preserve the historic character of Boston.

In our spiritual lives we also must take up a similar project—one that requires big digging. It is called the general examen of conscience. It is best not to wait until we are old, as did the city of Boston. The huge upheaval and overall nuisance of one deep dig can be prevented by what is aptly called "the preventive exam." This prayer helps us to know our needs beforehand, to recognize that falling in the same daily potholes suggests a danger below. In the preventive exam we scan the day that we will travel through and the day that travels through us. "What may happen today?" we ask, and "How am I likely to react?" We ask the Lord to pump up our virtues, keep us alert to needs and opportunities, and fill us with his grace.

> *To you belong the heavens; the earth, too, belongs to you; the universe with all it contains is your very own foundation.*
> *(Ps 89:12)*

And you

Make the preventive exam your morning prayer of readiness. It is as important as any other routine of the early hours. We need time to dress properly, eat breakfast, gather our things, leave the house on time, catch the bus or enter the traffic flow easily, and reach our destination ready for the day. We also need to wake our soul, nourish it, groom it, and set it off in the right direction. A little examination prayer will do the trick.

44

Inheritance Prayer

Prayer

Kids watch the same shows over and over with endless delight. And if the show is a home video starring them, their delight knows no bounds. Even big kids, middle aged and older, enjoy seeing themselves immortalized. What a wonderful way to keep important concepts front and center: we are family, we share our joys, we support each other.

We can also relive faith moments. How often do you recall your baptism, for example? "Why would I want to?" you may ask. "I was a baby and all I did was cry." Well, *that* is memorable! You were just born and already being born again. That is certainly reason to cry out. Your baptism day really is worthy of a joyful shout if you think about what happened. At that moment, your parents gave you the greatest thing they had: the gift of faith. They stood before the Church and said: "We want our precious child to be fully prepared and outfitted for life, here and hereafter. We want our child to be ransomed from sin and clothed in grace." And so you were washed in saving waters, anointed a child of God, and joined to the great family of Christ, entitled to a lifetime of sacramental grace and an eternity of joy.

Throughout our lives we rely on that moment. As faithful Catholics, we have fully bought into our parents' dream, entrusting ourselves to this life of grace, believing in its efficacy, and living by its standards. But do we pray our baptism? The renewal prayer is a very simple and familiar one: the Sign of the Cross. On entering and leaving church we bless ourselves using holy water, which can be kept at home as well, or bless ourselves without it. Either way, it is the prayer that counts most.

"Go, therefore, and make disciples of all nations, baptizing them in the name of the Father and of the Son and of the Holy Spirit." (Mt 28:19)

And you

At baptism our life was given to God; when we sign ourselves with the cross we offer our life here and now to God. We pray: *In the name of the Father, and of the Son, and of the Holy Spirit. Amen.* I stand with the Blessed Trinity; I wear their colors, so to speak. My life belongs to them. What I do, I do with them, in their name, with their blessing. Amen.

45

Home-Cooked Prayer

Prayer

"We are what we eat!" How often the health-conscious offer this admonition. We hear it said less often that *we are what we pray*. Everyone knows the necessity of eating, and eating sensibly. Our life and its quality depend on sufficient nourishment, wisely chosen. And if this is true of the body, it is also true of the soul. Our spiritual works require upkeep as much as does our physical being. If you ever eat "on the run," at your desk (hopefully not while behind the wheel), you know you can satisfy your hunger easily enough, but you may not get much nutritional value. A good, balanced, home-cooked meal will nourish you so much more. Not the least reason for this is the calm and comfort factor.

Can our spirit be expected to thrive on a few crumbs sporadically tossed its way? And hopefully, it is not being filled with pure junk, which is so readily available all around us. No, the spirit too requires what Isaiah (25:6) calls "rich food and good wine." We should allow our soul at least one "real" meal every day. Whether we pray using a book or not, take at least fifteen minutes a day to speak (that is, pray) to God. Be sincere, be earnest, be attentive. Speak to the Divine Friend, remain open to his word, and then dine sumptuously on God's fare.

Whether you eat or drink or whether you don't, do everything for the glory of God. (1 Cor 10:31)

And you

If you want to know how you are doing spiritually, listen to your table conversation, that is, listen to *what* you pray. Are you a good companion, grateful for what is served, complimentary to the divine Cook? Make a point of feeding well both body and soul today.

46

The Prayer Compass

Prayer

Whenever we set out, we need a direction. We intend to get from here to there. Our prayers need direction, too: from me to God.

Before the invention of the GPS, we relied on a compass to go from here to there. As we know, a compass has five points. Yes, five! North, South, East, West, *and* where you are. Before heading in any direction, we should know where we are.

Prayer has four destinations: adoration, contrition, thanksgiving, and supplication. (The acronym ACTS, formed from these names, saved me many times in religion class.) These four are also known as the forms, purposes, or the ends of prayer because all prayers fall naturally into one of them. We adore God, ask his pardon, thank him, and ask favors of him. Our prayers always head in at least one of these four directions. Prayer, then, radiates out from you in four directions. We could easily say that these four *encompass* all of our prayer. It goes from my heart to the heart of God, from where I'm at, from my present frame of mind, my distraction, my preoccupation, my degree of attraction, to God.

In a sense, this is our response to Saint Paul's invitation to measure up to the dimensions of God.

> *May Christ dwell in your hearts through faith, firmly rooted and established in love, so that with all the saints you may be able to understand the breadth, the length, the height, and the depth, and know Christ's love which surpasses all knowledge so that you may be filled with all God's fullness. (Eph 3:17–19)*

When will we ever go overboard in adoration? How contrite are we when we no longer need to ask for mercy? When we thank him, God will never say "enough." Neither does he ever tire of hearing us ask for things. In other words, prayer has no limit.

> *Grace has been given to each of us according to the extent of Christ's gift. (Eph 4:7)*

And you

What direction do you favor in prayer? Try taking a couple of steps in each direction every day so that you will be more aware of where you are.

47

Running Water

Prayer

On a frigid weekend when I was thirteen a department store in town burned down. The fire started late Sunday night. When I passed by the site on Monday morning on the way to school, ice completely covered the intersection. Walking was slow and treacherous. I saw fire engines every where as well as emergency personnel and policemen who tried to keep curious pedestrians at bay. During the late hours of battle, the hydrants had been supplying torrents of water to quench the blaze. At a certain point, as the newspapers reported, the water supply froze on the pavement and in the hoses. The fire destroyed the store and all it contained.

The saving grace of water had shut off and the fire took over with such violence that the firemen had to stand back. Our battles with passion end the same way when the flow of grace is impeded. We may find ourselves completely cold toward anything religious. We feel everything outside of religion is warm and sunny and free, while church and prayer, and even God himself, are cold, distant, and oppressive. What happened to our early love? Scripture asks this same question of the members of the early churches (see Rev 2:2–7). Most of us started out enchanted by the fatherly God who watched over us. We prayed from our hearts back then. Perhaps "back then" lasted until just recently, when the fire of our passions rose up. They threatened our entire structure. Were we able to open the faucet of grace? Perhaps as an adult Christian we had not kept up on "paying" our utility bills, and thus we cut off the precious supply of grace. Prayer must also grow up in order to sustain our needs as adults. Keep up to date in your spiritual life. Pray for the present.

> *If what you heard from the beginning does remain in you, you'll also remain in fellowship with the Son and with the Father. And this is the promise he gave to you—life everlasting. (1 Jn 2:24–25)*

And you

Take a little walk down your spiritual memory lane. Revisit memories and impressions of your young days of fervor. What did your parents, grandparents, or other adults teach you about prayer? What did you learn in religious instruction? What was your favorite prayer or religious practice? Have you kept any mementos from your childhood faith? Are you able to update your devotion in order to live it again today?

48

Inner Traffic

Prayer

Sometimes when I am praying, I realize my mental channel has suddenly switched. It's not a matter of falling asleep and dreaming, but of glazing over and suffering a kind of electrical interference. While reflecting on some sublime reality, I suddenly realize that my mind is elsewhere (perhaps with my inability to locate a particular book or the price of canned lunch meat). In analyzing this, the problem seems to be low battery, or, more precisely, not enough sleep. Normally, however, the greatest impediment to prayer is nothing more serious than distraction. And we know distraction doesn't require any particular cause; it just happens.

Our places of prayer are often on the busiest city streets. It's amazing how the cacophony of honking horns, screeching tires, and blaring radios are so much less distracting than the little voices of internal traffic. The saints recommend leaving worries and preoccupations at the church door to be picked up again upon leaving. Perhaps those of us who are still saints-in-training don't have this option. For us, these distractions and temptations are like unruly children who have accompanied us to prayer, always fidgeting and fussing. They may require a glance, a reassuring pat, or a gentle reprimand to settle down. And when our distractions create what my mother called "an infernal ruckus," we may just have to take them in hand right then and there. Sometimes an inner distraction just needs to be acknowledged and it will quiet down.

Then we have external distractions: the unconscious drumming on a nearby pew, a jangling rosary, rustling of paper, doors squeaking, and someone *has* fallen asleep and is snoring. And the cell phone! *Why don't people turn off their phones . . . ? I'm here for a few moments of quiet prayer, but the noise is unbearable.* And just then you realize that the loud, very unreligious ringtone is coming from your own phone!

Perhaps all our distractions just need to be prayed. Who knows better than the Lord how much they are a part and parcel of our lives?

> But you, O Lord, are a shield around me, my glory, and the one who lifts up my head. (Ps 3:3)

And you

Next time you feel burdened by a distraction, try adding it to your prayer. You might say: "Lord, this thought won't leave me and I am so preoccupied by these other things, can I just talk with you about them?"

49

Connecting Prayer

Prayer

Many employers allow a dress-down day on which workers can come in their most comfortable attire. However, comfortable is often not very attractive, and the concept itself isn't altogether clear. Is it to promote a feeling of belonging and *ownership*, or is it meant as a statement of independence?

Camaraderie is good, and most of us enjoy those long, leisurely conversations over a cup of coffee at the local shop. We can also arrange to spend a couple of hours on the phone with a friend. Then we devote time to chats online, to texting, and sometimes to mindless connecting.

Who would take us seriously if we dashed into a room, blurted out something earth-shattering, then turned and dashed out again? We want our big news to have a hearing; we want that moment of sheer joy or sorrow to be heard, absorbed, and responded to—properly! *No distraction, please! Are you really listening to me? Do you hear what I'm saying?* Are we just as insistent with God, wanting to connect, to be certain he is listening, that he cares enough to at least acknowledge our presence? Find time for leisurely prayer, detailed and trusting. And if you are a good listener in turn, the Lord may confide in you. He also is saddened by concerns *and* has good news to share, if we are there to listen.

And he said to them,
"Consider what you hear.
With the measure you measure, it will be measured out
    to you,
and more will be added as well.
For whoever has,
to him it shall be given.
And whoever does not have,
even what he has will be taken from him." (Mk 4:24–25)

And you

It is not that Jesus will confide in you only if you are open and honest with him. However, you are not likely to even notice or recognize his attempts unless you are used to his inner voice. This familiarity comes only to the open ear, to the heart that anticipates the Lord's approach. If we glide on autopilot, as a rule it is easier to lose interest and drift away than to grow more enthusiastic. So if you are anxious to be heard by the Lord, speak up: often and insistently. He longs to be your Best Friend.

50

Childish Ways

Prayer

When we were children we recognized love as giving. Not that we were so giving, except with affectionate hugs and kisses, but we knew we were loved by how much was given to us. For our parents this meant how much they willingly gave up for us. If the funds were low, the treats were only for the children; if someone had to give in on a weekend activity, it was usually the parents. Who sacrificed sleep for a childhood illness? Who didn't watch the ballgame to play catch with a budding pitcher? We knew we were loved because of the many ways our parents gave of themselves. Now that we are the grown ups, we do the extra little loving things for the children in our lives.

In the spiritual life, God is the parent par excellence, constantly giving of himself. He has given us a whole universe of beauty to behold, as well as all the personal gifts of nature through our parents, grace through his Church, and gifts of circumstance in where we live, what we do, and who we're with. His greatest gift, of course, is his Son, in whom we see the Father's love and experience his generosity in the free gift of salvation. God sent his Son to live among us and to die for our sins. With all of that we are still the possessors of a childish love: we smile sweetly at God, the loving Father. But how rarely do we act as the true son or daughter? As adult Christians are we able to put ourselves in the position of giver? Do we look for ways to be signs of God's love and generosity to others? Are we willing to suffer something for the good of another?

> *When I was a child I spoke like a child, thought like a child, reasoned like a child. When I became a man, I put an end to childish ways. (1 Cor 13:11)*

And you

The biggest responsibility of the adult believer is to do the will of God. It is not the easiest thing to recognize in our complicated existence, but discern we must in order to take our place as sons and daughters of God. Look at the responsibilities of your present life and pray for the gift of discernment to know and to correspond to God's will for you each day.

51

Downright Difficult

Prayer

In recent years television has become saturated with reality shows. We've followed plus-sized people losing unbelievable amounts of weight, hunters searching for the most dangerous animals on our planet, and adventurers competing to be the first to safely reach an exotic destination. Many of these activities rank high on the danger scale. They may require extreme daring and are downright difficult! But some persons would still prefer these contests to the simple act of praying.

Prayer, they say, is too difficult! By this they may mean too scary or too troubling. Or they may style themselves self-made with no need of God. They may be willing to face any physical challenge with gusto, but they have never stepped inside their own soul.

Jesus, who frequented the synagogue to pray with others, gave us the model of belonging, engaging in worship as a church community. He gathered friends and taught them how to pray. As social beings, we are meant to approach God as a family, not just go it on our own.

However, no matter our relationship with organized religion, God remains *our* God. Totally for us! The New Testament is full of images and impressions of God, of his love and concern for each of us. He is the Good Shepherd, the father of the wayward son, the mother hen, welcomer of the sinful woman, Peter's forgiver.

"Everyone who has a heart possesses all that is necessary for prayer. It is enough to give one's heart to God," says Blessed James Alberione. We do not need words or even sentiments to approach God. The slightest movement toward him *is* prayer.

> *"How often I wished to gather your children, the way a hen gathers her brood under her wings, but you would not!" (Mt 23:37)*

And you

Have confidence. God is anxious to hear your voice. Prayer is no time for reservation. Speak with the confidence you have toward a good friend who provides an attentive ear, an open heart, and a guarantee of confidentiality. We relax our defenses with a friend, and we tend to accept a friend's advice more easily because of our own trust. If you find the idea of prayer unnerving, try this: get a cup of coffee, pull up a chair as you would with a friend, and simply chat with God.

52

Praying the News

Prayer

In California I lived in a house of flowers. Semi-exotic plants filled our patio. But with the least bit of water, grassy weeds appeared. Their seeds, blown in through the patio walls or carried by birds, certainly weren't sown by a cunning enemy such as Jesus spoke of (see Mt 13:24–28). In the garden parable, the Evil One sowed weeds among the wheat.

Sowing weeds is really nothing new. Jesus told us not to jump to conclusions at the report of bad news. On hearing of those killed by a falling tower, he asked, "Do you think they were guiltier than everyone else living in Jerusalem?" (Lk 13:4)

We are experienced enough with media reporting to recognize sensationalism even in mainstream coverage. Speculation runs rampant, especially in unauthorized and unsubstantiated comments. We may wish there was only good news to share, but bad news—tragedy, cruelty, and sin—is a fact. Sin is news—not good news, but it is news. Every day we flick on channels or pick up a newspaper only to read of war, gun violence, lying, cheating, stealing, and selfishness of all sorts. But we hear good news as well, news about selfless civil servants, "Good Samaritans," and persons who place themselves in danger to protest injustice.

In whatever form it takes, we cannot afford to ignore the news because it is happening in God's good world; it is happening to our brothers and sisters; and it is our responsibility, too, since we are one with Christ, the Redeemer. We may be able to influence some situations in some ways, but our basic duty is to pray. We are the pray-ers of the people, the pray-ers of the news.

"Love your enemies, and pray for those who persecute you, so that you'll become sons of your Father in Heaven, because he causes his sun to rise on the evil and the good, and rain to fall on the just and the unjust." (Mt 5:44–45)

And you

It is so easy and normal to focus all our pity on the victims in a news story, but as Christians, our prayers, if not our hearts, should reach out to both the innocent and the guilty. How do you react to the news? Is your first thought of prayer for all those involved? Remember that announcers, producers, media personnel, and advertisers need prayers too.

53

You've Got the Power!

Prayer

In our age of high-tech devices, high-energy drinks, and high-impact workouts, being powerful seems normal. However, now we are concerned with a different type of power. Blessed James Alberione, a modern spiritual master, said that "a great power both for the present life and for the future life is at the disposal of everyone. Everything depends on whether or not it is used, and used well. This power is prayer."

How is prayer a power when it so often seems childish and distracted? Its secret power lies in its source. A famous saying about prayer puts it like this: *Pray as if everything depended on you and trust as if everything depended on God.* Basically that says it all. On our part, we need humility, confidence, and perseverance. Humility requires us to address God as the One with the power, and self as the one with the need. Confidence believes that God wants to answer our prayers and that he will do it. Perseverance keeps us coming back.

We do not need a special way to express ourselves when we pray. God understands. And for his part, God inspires and empowers our prayer. God often addresses people in a very human way. Think of his conversations with Abraham (see Genesis) or Moses (see Exodus and Deuteronomy), or with Peter or Paul (see Acts). They conversed about what was important at the moment. Sometimes God had a request, as when he invited Abraham to leave his father's land and set out where God would direct him. At other times God is very attentive to our requests. He rescued both Peter and Paul from imprisonment and often helped them to make decisions in their ministry.

We have the power and it is this: prayer, which is always a conversation with our God. And our God is a loving Father who waits to hear of all our concerns.

> *"And now we've all come together here in God's presence to hear all that you've been commanded by the Lord." (Acts 10: 33)*

And you

Recall one or two things that you have fretted over lately. Blessed James Alberione said we should feel familiar enough with God even to tell him when our shoes make our feet hurt. Perhaps you feel helpless, powerless in the face of your concerns. Bring them now to God in a prayerful conversation. Explain your situation and ask for his help.

54

Pharisee Within

Prayer

The problem with being a hypocrite is that it's only obvious to everyone else. The poor hypocrite is in the dark. Besides that, hypocrites don't mean to be hypocrites. They are generally well-meaning people who hyperventilate over what others should be doing while themselves living by rules of their own. A most impressive example is found in François Mauriac's *Pharisienne* (*The Woman of the Pharisees*). Madame Brigitte Plan lived on the front lines of faith. She was the go-to person in her village, the doyenne of right living who took it upon herself to keep everyone on the straight and narrow. In the course of right-doing, unknown to herself, Madame Brigitte became embittered, interfering, and driven. In the wake of her perfection lay the ruined lives of her husband, the parish priest, and various neighbors. Eventually she came to recognize what she had become, but this recognition also fell victim to her unfortunate bent. She now saw that never had anyone done as much harm as she had done, and never had anyone been as sorry. Even in repentance the good Madame had to be the gold standard. Sad as this is, she was consistent and not entirely unusual.

This is a point of contention for many: What is the proper place for one's religion? Should our piety be "out there" or should it remain behind closed doors? The answer lies in the middle. If my heart belongs to God, it will be obvious by who I am. I will not have to walk the streets wearing a sandwich board proclaiming my position. I will not have to, nor have time to, always appear hands folded, knees bent. But neither will I insist it is enough that God knows I am his. Sanctity (how I stand with God) and piety (how I stand before God and others) are not easily misrepresented. We either are or aren't holy and pious. We are either real or phony. God knows and that is all that really matters.

"For with the judgment you judge,
you will be judged.
And with the measure you measure,
it will be measured out to you." (Mt 7:2)

And you

Sincerity gives an example to others without even trying. Do you know the difference between concern that others live their faith and interference? Pray for the ability to observe and discern, especially your own motivations.

55

What Does Prayer Do?

Prayer

What does prayer do? That is a tricky question. Prayer doesn't actually *do* anything in our common way of defining accomplishment. Prayer is not automatically answered. It is not like a coin-operated dispensing machine: *Insert your prayer in the slot marked A, and pick up your answer at slot B.*

The important point is what prayer *is.* Prayer is a relationship between me and God. So what prayer does, we could say, is how it affects us. It makes us more receptive, more open, available, and understanding of God's plans for us.

Suppose I am praying that my acne clears up for my date this weekend. Perhaps I will be inspired to try a certain cream that will cure me. However, God may want to show me that my personality is more than my appearance. I can be liked and even loved for who I am. "What I keep praying for," you say, "is bigger than that. I want world peace!" Ah, yes, and the world continues to torment itself with wars, turmoil, and distrust. So what happened to all the prayers said by you and so many others for this elusive peace? They went directly to the heart of God. God treasures those prayers because they are bigger than your wants and needs. However, world peace is in the power of humanity. God will not take back the authority he gave to human hands at creation. But he will bless the efforts of the human family to live in peace. And to those who beg for peace, God will give the gift of inner peace, a harmony of spirit with God and his desires. So whether I pray for myself or for someone else, for something urgent or useful, what prayer *does* is enhance my union with God. It fills me with awe and gratitude that God has such concern for me that he listens and hears.

> *"Peace I leave with you,*
> *my peace I give to you;*
> *not as the world gives*
> *do I give to you." (Jn 14:27)*

And you

Take some time to look closely at how you pray for what you want or feel you need. If you find that the great Vending Machine in the sky isn't doling out positive replies, you may want to revisit Whom you are dealing with. God's response is more personalized than you can imagine.

~~~~~~~ *56* ~~~~~~~~~~~~~~~~~~~~~~~~~~~~~~~~~~~~

Emergency Kit

Prayer

Every kitchen, classroom, workplace, and car needs a well-stocked emergency kit. When we need a Band-Aid, we often need to grab one quickly. If you have to give a big presentation to your employer in five minutes and you get a nasty paper cut from your notes, only a Band-Aid will do. You can't show up in the conference room with a tissue tied around the cut. And it is impractical to think of keeping that hand hidden in your pocket the whole time (especially if you have no pocket).

In life all different kinds of emergencies crop up. They range from the minor annoyance of a missing sock to the terror of an earthquake. We do not dwell on the possibility of these disasters. We brush aside catastrophic events—asteroids and the like. The disaster *du jour* is more likely to be a relationship spinout, an escalating verbal exchange, or a fire stoked by insult and innuendo. Too often conversation can devolve into a shouting match, cruel words, hateful accusations, broken hearts, and ruined relationships. No Band-Aid will staunch these wounds. In fact, trying to slap a Band-Aid over them is the worst thing we could do.

These emergency situations require more than just a well-stocked kit. In these triage situations, everyone involved is wounded. So take one big breath in, breathe one sincere prayer out. Prayer provides the necessary time-out, the chance to reflect. Assess the wound and treat it, even if you can only take charge of your own heart.

> *The LORD is building up Jerusalem;*
> *he reunites the exiles of Israel.*
> *He heals the broken-hearted*
> *and binds up their wounds. (Ps 147:2–3)*

And you

Keeping prayer at hand is a vital necessity. It is like the 911 call that brings help to life's emergencies. Prayer can staunch any wound and revive the lifeless spirit. Assess your prayer emergency kit. Are you well prepared?

57

Cleanliness

Prayer

Cleanliness is next to godliness. Most likely we've all heard this pious catchphrase at one time or other. For me it always conjures up images of supermarkets—*go down aisle 16-B and you'll find cleanliness right next to godliness.*

It also makes me think of my beloved computer. I have always attributed its slowness to a bad attitude, but the technician recently told me it has a memory problem. Poor computer has so much in its big square head, it can't store one more itsy-bitsy file without a fuss.

This is an all too common prayer problem, too. To pray well we need free space in the soul (that is, the mind, heart, and will). We fret a lot about the outer atmosphere of our prayer. We want this outer space to be quiet, calm, recollected, and full of holy candle scents. But what about our inner atmosphere?

To be clean of heart, as Jesus advises in the Sermon on the Mount (see Mt 5), means cleanliness of soul. It means we are so zeroed in on godliness that we do not absorb much of the frivolity around us. We do not clog up our memory with every electronic or printed word ever uttered, and, even more so, we avoid what is commonly called "dirt," that is, pornography, hard core or cultural, which doesn't sit well with godliness. Just as in computers the muck mixes into all the files and corrupts them, so our best efforts at prayer will be undermined by this kind of infiltration.

God doesn't expect us to exist in a vacuum. God has asked us to involve ourselves in the crying needs of the world around us. Being on the same page as God—godliness—is a boon to our spirits. These concerns provide fuel for our prayer. Rule of thumb for folded hands: If what rises to mind in prayer embarrasses, it won't fit between cleanliness and godliness.

"You purify the outside of the cup and the plate,
but inside they're full of greed and self-indulgence." (Mt
23:25)

And you

When you decide to pray, do you find the files of your mind and heart clogged by many unnecessary notions and news notes? Make a decision, for the good of your prayer, to guard against junk that so easily invades and corrupts your best efforts.

Prayer Patterns

Prayer

In one of my first jobs, I worked in a shop. Besides sales, the job included cleaning duties. The manager had some peculiarities, one of these being that the floor had to be swept in a particular pattern. The edge by the walls had to be swept first, followed by broom strokes toward the middle. The pattern resembled the spokes of a wagon wheel. To this day I am not sure why this was the schema for sweeping, but it was what it was. To some people Catholic prayer patterns are just as disconcerting. Why does the Mass, for example, have to always be the same? Our prayer seems rote and boring.

The first thing to remember is that prayer comes in different forms. Our own personal prayers said privately can be as flamboyant as we like: between God and us. Liturgical prayer, on the other hand, follows a particular pattern. There is a good reason for this sameness. You might ask: Why do we have a tune and set words for the common Happy Birthday song? Well, first to facilitate a group celebration; and second, to aid our memory. Generally a group sings the song to the person celebrating. Likewise, the pattern of the prayers used to celebrate the Mass is always the same. Since each Mass is the renewal of the sacrifice Jesus made, each Mass needs to be authentically celebrated. To ensure this, the prayers and gestures follow set formulas. In fact, wherever we go in the world, and whatever language is spoken, the Mass is being celebrated using the same prayers and gestures.

Some folks get lost in the sameness. They find Mass uninspiring, claiming that they get nothing out of it. However, to get something out of it, they need to put something into it. Liturgical prayer calls out for participation. It is true that sometimes the way a Mass is *celebrated* is uninspiring, but the event taking place is very important. Jesus, through his priest and together with us, is offering the sacrifice of his life for our redemption. It is the same sacrifice first offered on Calvary renewed again. Why? Because it is the most important event in human history and it calls for continual celebration.

For with one offering he [Jesus] has perfected forever those who are being sanctified. (Heb 10:14)

And you

Are you annoyed by the sameness of Sunday liturgies, or the dullness of how liturgy may be celebrated? How much do you understand about what is taking place? What effort have you personally put into your participation at Mass?

59

Just a Drop

Prayer

We often hear complaints about the obligation to attend Mass. We attend because we are Catholics and it is the principal act of Catholic worship. "I don't get anything out of it, but at least I go," say some. If this is your problem, too, how do you identify with it? Do you understand what is happening at the altar? Do you try to place yourself where you can see and hear well? Do you pick up a missalette and read the comments about the actions and activities that are taking place?

The Mass, or the Eucharistic Celebration, is an entire tableau of our salvation. We enter the house of God as sinners, asking to be forgiven so as to participate worthily. We listen to the readings, which recount parts of the story of salvation. When we pray the Creed, we acknowledge our belief in the sacred mysteries of God. We pray together in the Universal Prayer for the needs of the human family, the Church, our own family, and ourselves. We offer God the bread and wine received from his goodness and from the work of those who made them. We join with the priest in the great prayer of praise and petition called the Canon or Eucharistic Prayer, the central section that culminates in the consecration of the bread and wine into the Body and Blood of Jesus Christ. The prayers continue until, together with Jesus and all Christians everywhere, we pray the Our Father. After once more professing our unworthiness, we process to the altar to receive the Body and Blood of Christ in Holy Communion. A time of thanksgiving follows, then a final prayer and blessing from the priest. We are sent out to bring the love of Christ to our everyday lives and activities.

> *Therefore, let us confidently approach the throne of grace to receive mercy and find grace to help us in time of need. (Heb 4:16)*

And you

Choose a part of the Mass to concentrate on each week. You might start with the Presentation of the Gifts, when the bread and wine are brought to the altar where the priest offers them as gifts to God. Pay attention as the priest pours a drop of water into the chalice of wine. This mingling of water and wine represents the humanity and divinity of Christ. Let it also symbolize the offering of yourself. Add your life, your concerns, troubles, disappointments, and sacrifices to the great chalice of Christ's sacrifice.

60

The Inside Story

Prayer

A story is told about a little boy who was often found standing on his chair at the dinner table. His parents said to him, "Son, please sit down on your chair." He did sit, but moments later up he popped. "Please sit down" was said so many times that the *please* wore thin and disappeared. Soon he was hearing the same command that Fido learned in obedience school: "Sit!" Combining this with a few stern looks did the trick. The little boy stayed seated at table, but looking up at his parents, he solemnly announced, "I'm standing up on the inside."

Have you ever found yourself doing something similar at prayer? Our liturgies have rubrics (the how-to's of celebration, what is done when). Our celebrations have a variety of stances and gestures. We sit for readings and announcements; we stand for the Gospel proclamation and for certain prayers; we trace a small cross on our forehead, lips, and heart before the Gospel reading; we turn and shake hands with those around us; we kneel at the consecration when the bread and wine become the Body and Blood of Christ; we make the Sign of the Cross to begin and end the Mass. These are some of our common expressions of prayer.

Sometimes it may happen that everyone, perhaps including yourself, is kneeling, but your heart is prostrate on the floor in adoration. At another time we all bow our heads to pray, "Lord, have mercy; Christ, have mercy." Your soul, meanwhile, is clinging to Christ who hangs on the cross before you. And sometimes, when the Church community is silently standing in prayer, your heart is joyfully twirling and dancing for God.

> *O LORD, you have searched me and known me.*
> *You know when I sit down and when I rise up. (Ps 120:1–2)*

And you

What did Saint Hildegard of Bingen say? "Do not be listless in celebrating, but rather be on fire with enthusiasm." We do not suggest breaking ranks during the liturgy to cartwheel down the main aisle, but a soul on fire will participate with enthusiasm, which will carry over into one's words and deeds after the celebration. Although you may feel bogged down by personal reluctance or cultural reserve, God sees into your heart. He sees your spontaneity and love, and, no doubt, he is pleased.

61

You Had Me at Hallow

Prayer

Our Father, who art in heaven, hallowed be thy name.

Normally I try to spend a few minutes in thanksgiving after daily Mass. One day I was startled out of my supposed recollection when I overheard myself pray: "God bless you, Lord." At the same moment I'm pretty sure I heard muffled laughter from above. Either my sacred synapses had snapped or I was more preoccupied than I care to admit. On later reflection, however, I realized that there isn't much we can offer God more appropriate than a blessing.

God loves our every word directed his way. Just as a parent is enthralled by baby's first babbling conversation, so God is all ears when we speak to him—no matter how incoherent our prayer. We could read the phone book to him and he would be divinely pleased. The secret is that *we* read it, pray it, and say it *to* him.

Praise is a precious commodity not shared nearly enough. Praise is what we *can* give God. It endears us to him. Jesus, who knows this better than anyone, built praise into the prayer he taught his disciples. They requested a formula so that they could pray as they had witnessed Jesus praying. The first line of the Lord's Prayer is precisely this: *hallowed be thy name.* May your name, O God, be made holy, or, more properly, holier. God's name is already all-holy, but our prayer is a blessing, wishing that God's name may be holier yet.

Hallowing God's name will spill over onto us. This holy spillage comes to us as grace that is the life, the holiness, of God. We, too, are destined to be hallowed, to become saints. Just think of the saved holy souls in purgatory. We celebrate with them on days like Halloween, the Holy Eve of All Saints' Day, and again on November 2, All Souls' Day.

> *Join me in celebrating the greatness of the LORD, and let us extol his name together. (Ps 34:4)*

And you

Imagine ways in which you can hallow God's name. If the name of God is to be held in esteem, so must the individual names of the Holy Trinity: Father, Son, and Holy Spirit. And again, by extension, we consider our name as Christian to be holy. In what ways do you hallow God's name?

62

Whatever He Wills

Prayer

Thy kingdom come; thy will be done on earth as it is in heaven.

Most of us have only a romantic notion of kings and kingdoms, so the first half of this phrase means less than the second half, which speaks of the will. The word *will* evokes thoughts of the will of the people, or that somehow God wills on earth exactly what we do.

Some spiritual writers have suggested that we take an attribute of God to emulate. I often tease my companions that my choice is this: "He does whatever he wills" (see Ps 115:3). And all too often I have thought it would be heavenly if I could say: "She (meaning me) does whatever she wills," with impunity, of course.

In reality, however, only God's will is right and just. This is so because God is the beautiful combination of all-knowing and all-loving. In other words, he knows what is best as well as the outcome of every action, and he only acts out of love. And all that God wills is aimed toward his kingdom, which is coming. When? When the time is right by God's wise judgment, the kingdom of God will be revealed. Why, then, do we pray that it happen? We pray each word of the Lord's Prayer because Jesus gave it to his disciples when they asked him to teach them how to pray. Jesus wants his Father's kingdom to come, and he knows that doing God's will is the road leading there. So, in fact, we are praying for our own salvation. And we are praying with and for all other people that they, too, may enter God's heavenly kingdom.

We are praying also that our lives, our families, our community, our country, our world will somehow take on a bit of the kingdom of heaven. First of all, that God may reign on our earth, that his rules would be our law, that we would all treat one another as do the angels and saints dwelling together in heaven.

The LORD brings about anything he pleases
in heaven and on earth,
in the sea and in whatever depths. (Ps 135:6)

And you

Have you ever plotted to have something go your way only to regret it later? What looks best from our vantage point may cause disasters down the line. Thank God ahead of time for his will in your regard.

63

Daily Bread

Prayer

Give us this day our daily bread.

I was one of those kids who ate anything that wasn't nailed down, so no one had to urge me to finish my food with stories of other kids around the world who would go to bed hungry. My parents always made sure we had enough to eat. Only the good Lord knows what was missing to make this possible. To make ends meet, my awesome Mom would mix a lot of powdered milk, frequent discount stores, and buy only day-old bread. "Tastes perfectly fine," she'd say, "and it only costs ten cents a loaf."

Our daily bread, or maize, or rice is important not only in itself as nourishment, but also in what it symbolizes to us: all is well; I'll be okay. Several times in the Gospels Jesus makes sure that those around him had sufficient food for the day. Twice he multiplied bread for the large crowd gathered to hear him preach (Mk 6:30–44; 8:1–10); he instructed his hungry companions to pluck and eat grain as they passed through fields (Lk 6:1–5); he fixed breakfast for his friends who had been fishing all night (Jn 21:9–13); and he began his ministry multiplying wine for a young couple's wedding banquet (Jn 2:2–11).

Not only did Jesus feed our bodies, but he also prepared abundant food to nourish our spirits. As he said in his own regard: "I have food to eat that you don't know about" (Jn 4:32). And later on, he declared: "My food is to do the will of the One who sent me" (Jn 4:34). Even beyond this, Jesus gave us the daily bread of the Eucharist, his own Body and Blood, as real food and real drink.

God provides for this basic need of daily sustenance for our bodies (food and drink), our spirits (the word of God in Scripture), and our souls (by daily Communion with his Body and Blood).

"I am the bread of life;
whoever comes to me will not hunger,
and whoever believes in me will never thirst." (Jn 6:35)

And you

Are you grateful for the abundant food that God places before you daily? Do you regularly feed your spirit on God's word by reading and reflecting on even just a short passage daily? Do you bless the Lord for the abundance of material food and drink available in our society? Is your heart open and your soul eager to receive Christ's Body and Blood, the bread of heaven, in Holy Communion?

64

No Trespassing!

Prayer

And forgive us our trespasses as we forgive those who trespass against us.

My community has a retreat house out in the country. Somehow it became the subject of a legend among local teens, who are collectively convinced that the house is haunted. Despite our *No Trespassing!* sign, on summer nights carloads of kids drive up, hop the fence, race to the front door, and dare each other to touch it. One night a particular Sister had had enough of this. As soon as the bravest knuckles reached for the wood, she whipped the door open. The shrieks and wheeling feet of the fleeing herd are now convent legend.

Most of us are familiar with the line in the Lord's Prayer: *And forgive us our trespasses as we forgive those who trespass against us.* What kind of trespassing does the prayer speak of? It is not referring to a lawn or porch, but to our personal inner space. What we don't want trampled on are our affections, our sensitivity, our privacy, our touchiness, our quirks, and so many other inner horizons.

In the Lord's Prayer we are making a high-stakes proposition. We are saying to God, "When you judge me, do it according to how I judge others. Forgive me only if, and as, I forgive those who have offended me." This is not a matter of spiritual bravado, but we are laying the fate of our souls across our own ability to forgive others.

It's a variation on the Golden Rule: Do unto others as you would have them do to you (see Lk 6:31). None of us are hoping that God will judge us by human standards. We look forward to divine mercy. *Lord, have mercy*, we often pray. If we bestow mercy, we will receive mercy. Mercy is a prayer. Let us attempt to cover all of our trespasses with the mercy we show.

> *"And whenever you stand in prayer, forgive whatever you have against anyone so that your Father in Heaven will also forgive you your offenses." (Mk 11:25)*

And you

How often do you pray the Lord's Prayer? If you save it only to be prayed at Mass on Sunday, it will not become the world-changing prayer Jesus meant it to be. Can you imagine the difference in your more challenging relationships if you learn to forgive as you hope to be forgiven?

65

Lead Us Not

Prayer

And lead us not into temptation, but deliver us from evil.

Some authors think that Judas, the apostle who betrayed Jesus, was really trying to spark the coming of God's kingdom. He accepted thirty pieces of silver to set up a situation where Jesus could be arrested. When this arrest took place, Judas expected Jesus to save himself through some impressive show of power. That didn't happen. But we don't know what Judas's motivation was for giving Jesus up to the authorities. Was he trying to help Jesus, or to get him out of the way? Either way, it was a terrible temptation.

We have temptations, too. While we like to take credit for inspirations to do good, for example, to give up our Saturday to help an elderly neighbor, to attend a parish retreat, or to join others in promoting a good cause, we quickly attribute temptations that lead to something questionable or evil to an outside influence. Nothing bad is ever our fault. Truthfully, temptations often originate outside of us: an attractive proposition, the suggestion of another person, or circumstances of the moment. One thing is certain: God never tempts us to evil. So when we pray in the Lord's Prayer (Our Father): "Lead us not into temptation, but deliver us from evil," we are actually begging the Lord to steer us clear of evil and even of anything that causes us to second-guess. *I'm not sure how this will turn out. It might get me in some trouble, but I'm going for it. It might not be good, but it's good for me right now.* Thoughts like this smack of temptation. People of prayer prefer to err on the side of prudence, to follow the better inspiration.

In giving us the Lord's Prayer, Jesus puts on our lips and in our hearts a request for assistance. *Help me, Lord, to recognize my weakness and to turn away from anything that could lead me away from you.*

> *The Lord is my shepherd, . . .*
> *He leads me in right paths. . . .*
> *Even though I walk through the darkest valley,*
> *I fear no evil;*
> *for you are with me. (Ps 23:1, 3–4, NRSV)*

And you

How honest are you about temptation? Can you see when a choice leads away from God? Can you trust Jesus, the Good Shepherd, to guide you through any difficulty or temptation? Make the Our Father your daily prayer.

66

Seal of Approval

Prayer

Amen.

England has many interesting customs. The British put little dresses, called cozies, on their teapots; they never stand in line for anything, but form a queue; they only allow men (or women) named Bobby to serve on the police force. (Sorry, I'm stretching it.) But one of my favorites is that certain products can sport a seal on their labels stating that they are the official jam, or ham, or laundry detergent of the crown. That is a rather classy seal of approval by any standard.

In a sense, God asks us to place a seal of approval on any prayer that we say. Almost any prayer, whether part of the liturgy or from a popular prayer book, or even one that originates in our own heart, is sealed by this one word: *Amen.* And this one little word, all by itself, is a prayer. It is like the prayer made by the father of a very sick little boy (see Mk

131

9:24) who cried out to Jesus, "I believe; help my unbelief!" Sometimes we have to substitute other words for *amen* in order to impress ourselves more deeply with its meaning: "I agree!" "I'm with you!" "May it be so." Our *amen*s should always be firm; we are not responding with "Whatever!"

You could argue that *amen* isn't even a real word. It's a *prayer word*. Where else do we use it but in our prayers? An adjective often employed in business discussions and legal transactions appears to be related. The word is *amenable*, in this sense meaning, *I can agree to that*. Our prayer word *amen* says the same thing: *I do agree with everything we just prayed. I am in accord.*

> Then all the angels stood around the throne, the elders, and the living creatures. They fell on their faces before the throne and worshipped God, saying:
>
> > "Amen! Blessing, glory, wisdom, thanks, honor,
> > power and might
> > be to our God forever and ever, amen!" (Rev 7:11–12)

And you

Some day each of us will say our last *amen*. How do you connect with this acclamation now? Reflect on your prayer life to see if you really believe what you are praying. One of the best ways to increase your faith is to repeat these words of Scripture: *I do believe. Help my unbelief.* Amen. So be it!

All's Fair

Prayer

"Mirror, mirror on the wall," cried Snow White's step-mother, "who is fairest of them all?" How often do we find ourselves checking our image in the mirror? For ladies it's the compact or restroom mirror; for gents it might be the rearview mirror or a towel bar. What are we looking for? Most likely we are dressed and our hair is still where we left it. What then are we looking for? It's the little things: a speck of food on a tooth, a hair out of place, mascara amiss, or dulled lip gloss. We may keep track of these, but they are not major moments in an otherwise wonderful day.

However, just as we check up on our outer appearance, so should we give a few glances at our inner self. In the morning we do the preventive exam as we prepare for the day, but we need spot checks here and there—usually midday and evening, to see how things are going. A little soul-searching.

Now, we shouldn't have to go hunting. We should know where our soul is at all times. (Hint: it's you!)

In these short prayerful checks, we can ask such things as: Have I been kind and thoughtful? Am I my usual cheerful self? If not, how have I failed? Have I sinned? Am I aware of having wronged anyone? This kind of check is called the examination of conscience. We make it at least twice a day to ensure that our best self is out and about. Then we only need a quick re-dab of charity to the lips, respect to the heart, uprightness to the will, and wisdom to the mind.

Just as these mirror checks of ourselves occasionally suggest a visit to the beautician or the barber, so our inner glances direct us regularly to the Sacrament of Reconciliation for a spiritual overhaul.

But you were washed clean, you were sanctified, you were admitted to fellowship with God in the name of the Lord Jesus Christ and by the Spirit of our God. (1 Cor 6:31)

And you

An interesting thing happens as you make these daily check-ups to examine the state of your soul before God. After a while you will become a mirror for others to do a little momentary self-check. Pray while making this exam that you will reflect the face of God to anyone who sees you.

68

Homely

Prayer

Let's hear it for old sweaters! Many of us have a favorite, comfortable old sweater. Along with a few holes and mismatched buttons, it carries around with it many memories. It can no longer be worn in public, but no matter! This sweater is homely; it is loved.

The word *homely* isn't used much as a compliment. In other English-speaking locales, however, we might be greeted with a heartfelt: "Make yourself homely, dear." In other words: "Make yourself at home."

This comfort factor needs a place in our prayer. If not all of our prayer feels *homely*, at least we should have a favorite prayer that we can always count on, a prayer that we can pull up at any time, anywhere—a warm, comfortable prayer that will ward off the ill winds and discomforts of life. This might be the Rosary, or the Divine Mercy Chaplet. It could be one of your own "home-made" prayers. The one I often say is the last stanza of the *Adoro Te Devote* by Saint Thomas Aquinas:

Jesus, whom for the moment veiled I see
What I so long for give to me
That I may one day see you face to face
And may be blessed your glory to embrace.

The wording is a little clumsy, but it's been with me so long it is like the old sweater of my soul. These lovely words speak to the most comfortable and comforting of devotions: Jesus Christ present in the Blessed Sacrament. He remains mysteriously in the consecrated wafers kept in the tabernacle specifically for our veneration. In this form, Jesus is veiled from our sight, but not from our faith. We find comfort and strength in this hidden company as we await his embrace in heaven.

"So you, too, are in grief now,
but I'll see you again
and your hearts will rejoice,
and no one will take your joy from you." (Jn 16:22)

And you

If you do not yet have a favorite, *homely* prayer, keep your eyes open for one. Meanwhile, take full advantage of the sentiments that hold vigil in your heart. You may want to make a habit of turning toward the nearest church to praise Jesus, thank him, adore him—and so close the distance between you and the Lord with the comfort of prayer.

―――― *69* ―――――――――――――――――――――――

You Are Here!

Prayer

We live in an exciting world. Although the planet itself is an antique, something unbelievably new is always happening. Just last week I read this headline: "An iceberg the size of Manhattan is about to calve!" Mother Nature is certainly a drama queen. She's always changing, becoming more complex.

As our life goes along and becomes more complex, prayer has to be reshaped. Life can gang up on our prayer and leave it whimpering. But remember, prayer is not what you prayed last month, or what you might pray tomorrow, it's what you're praying here and now. So it's important to recognize your present state. Some days you couldn't care less about prayer because your "here" is all messed up. Headache, heartache, difficulty, or doubt—whatever the reason, you are not into prayer. What to do? A wise person gave me this remedy: pray as you did when you were most fervent, when prayer meant

137

the most. *But that's insincere*, you might say. *It's phony!* No, it's practical. We practice and pretend for many things in life, sometimes at work, sometimes in our relationships. We even practice for sports, where motivation not mood dictates.

It's all part of the journey of prayer: the ups and downs, the pleasure and the pain. It is also the promise of prayer. If we could reach a plateau in prayer where every day's journey was level and smooth, it might become dull and boring. If things went splendidly every day, who's back would we pat? It is more healthy and realistic to expect our prayer to match our life—full of valleys and plains, mountains and mole-hills. We may even be progressing nicely in prayer, going ahead steadily like a train through the mountains when suddenly a landslide up ahead brings everything to a halt. What can we do? A little digging, perhaps, but mostly we have to wait patiently for the tracks to be cleared. When our fervor suffers a few dents and dings, our prayer has come into its own. Now our prayer begins to mirror our life and that is good. Our prayer becomes more part and parcel of who we are. *I* am praying, we can say.

> *Rejoice always, pray constantly, give thanks no matter what happens, for this is God's will for you in Christ Jesus. (1 Th 5:16–18)*

And you

Are you happy with how you pray? Keep a log of this week's prayers; watch yourself and see whether or not your prayer reflects your moods and needs.

No Pain, No Gain

Prayer

"If anything was more useful for our salvation than suffering, Christ would certainly have taught it to us by word and example" (*Imitation of Christ*, II, 12:15).

What does that quote mean? Who wants heaven if we can enter only through sufferings? "Bah, humbug!" It's enough to make us all into Ebenezer Scrooge in *A Christmas Carol* by Dickens.

Take a few moments to read those words again. This is Jesus speaking about suffering. If anyone in all of history knew about suffering, it was Jesus. We cannot be devoted only to the "dear Jesus" or to the "dude Jesus," that is, to the Jesus who preached and cured with a calm majesty, or to the Jesus who overturned the ideas and values of the wise men of his day. No one can live a life only on his own terms. Sometimes life is thrown at us; sometimes we have to struggle to get up from beneath the burdens of life; sometimes we have to patiently bear the jeers and insults life hurls at us. For some, life is literally a way of the cross, just like the one Jesus traveled from his condemnation to his crucifixion, a way of suffering that will end only in death. Isn't that totally useless, you ask? Of what possible benefit are pain, humiliation, suffering, and death?

The answer to the benefit of suffering can only be realized by gazing at the cross. Jesus came among us ultimately to offer his life for our salvation. That means he came to embrace suffering. And let's be honest: our life also will have its share of suffering. It is impossible to be a human being and not suffer. If we learn to see our own personal crosses through the lens of the saving sufferings of our Redeemer, our sufferings will gain a certain luster and the lightness that love alone can give.

"Those who want to be my followers, must deny themselves, pick up their cross, and follow me." (Mk 8:34)

And you

One of the most common devotions to the cross is to display a cross or crucifix in a prominent place at home. Being devoted to the crucified Christ has always been the honor of true Christians. Are you comfortable with this sign of your salvation?

I Am Cinderella!

Prayer

I fear I am a romantic. I've always loved those tales where a bad situation turns out splendidly, as with the story of Cinderella. Her step-family mistreated and undervalued her. She had no opportunities for advancement until the royal invitation arrived for a grand party at the palace. With the unlikely help of clever mice and a fairy godmother, Cinderella attended and enchanted the prince. Curfew dependent magic spells caused Cinderella to take the first coach back home, conveniently leaving a glass slipper behind. With great effort Prince Charming sought the girl who fit the slipper, and, against the craftiness of her sisters, Cindi gets her man. Isn't this how all of life's stories should end?

However, we know life doesn't follow the pattern of fairy stories. The invitation to a better life can get lost in the mail; the glass slipper may really fit the wrong gal; and the prince might not bother to find Cinderella.

For real life we need another model, something more than fairy tales, and we find it in the Gospel stories of Jesus. We can enter into these accounts and stand shoulder to shoulder with the various characters. For example, we can open the Gospel of John to chapter 20 and accompany Mary Magdalene to the tomb of Jesus. Feel her astonishment at finding the stone rolled away, her frustration at not seeing his body, her tears of helplessness and sorrow. Hear the familiar voice addressing her: "Mary!" Enter the story, walk around, talk to people, touch things, feel things that stir within you.

This is dynamic prayer, the true romantic prayer of contemplation. This is not simply pretending. By praying with Scripture in this way, we allow ourselves to become more familiar with the true Prince Charming, Jesus Christ. It is a perfect preparation for living your own Gospel stories, your daily interaction with Christ as he moves through the moments of your life.

> So they said to him, "Rabbi"—which, translated, means "Teacher"—"where are you staying?" "Come and you'll see," he said to them. (Jn 1:38–39)

And you

Choose favorite stories from the Bible and enter into them as you would enter a film or novel. With your imagination accompany the persons and events. Don't think of it as daydreaming or fantasy. It's a classic style of meditation taught by Saint Ignatius of Loyola. It is a proven way of bonding with Christ, which is the goal of our prayer.

~~~~~ 72 ~~~~~~~~~~~~~~~~~~~~~~~~~~~~~~~~

Just a Line

Prayer

Sometimes when we slit open an envelope, we find a card with a long, lovely verse followed by familiar handwriting: "Just a line to say hello, hope you are doing fine."

These few words contain much deeper sentiments and convey emotions shared many times before. Just that line, however, assures us of the love and attention of the sender.

Each chapter in this book offers just a line of Scripture related to the topic discussed. These lines from the word of God are short heralds of a larger message. We read into each of these lines the love, concern, compassion, and instruction of our God. Scripture is God speaking to whoever is reading his word. Each passage has a personal message for the reader. A useful practice is to savor these lines of Scripture either while reading the chapters or as a separate prayer practice at a later time. For example, in Chapter 64 of this book we read: "And whenever you stand in prayer, forgive whatever you have against anyone so that your Father in Heaven will also forgive you your offenses" (Mk 11:25).

It does happen, perhaps all too often, that we read Scripture quotes quickly and without much attention. We've heard these words before. I would suggest that you read the line slowly two or three times. Substitute the first *you* with your own name. *And, Lea, whenever you stand in prayer. . . .* Let the Lord speak to you personally with each of these lines of Scripture.

Then take a look at what is being said. Here the words seem to refer to the moment we stand before receiving Communion to say: *Lamb of God, you take away the sins of the world; have mercy on us.* Jesus tells us that we will have our sins taken away if we forgive whatever we have against anyone else. Jesus wants us to develop a heart as big as his own. We should do for others whatever we want done for us.

> *Now there are also many other things that Jesus did; if every one of them were written down, I don't suppose the world itself would have room for the books that would be written. (Jn 21:25)*

And you

Open to any chapter of this book and reread the line of Scripture. Ask yourself what you understand it to say. Quietly sit with it, asking the Lord to suggest to you his meaning. Consider writing a response to the line of Scripture.

73

Zen and Now

Prayer

Many people are looking for a way to relax and connect with their inner strengths. Stress seems to be the name of the game in our daily existence. It comes from work, relationships, inner conflict, and guilt, and it seems to be self-generating. We live in the midst of constant sound. Noise blares everywhere: traffic, play grounds, arguments, loud music. For some even the much-touted workout as a means to relieve stress doesn't bring the desired peace and calm. We could complain from here to eternity, but complaints don't generate the peace for which we yearn.

Many folks have turned to Eastern mysticism because those who espouse it appear so peaceful. Zen, for example, teaches the art of emptying as a means to peace. Although this may bring calming, centering, and soothing to the human spirit, it doesn't bring about connecting.

An innocent deception is happening. Has the spirit been cleared or merely anesthetized? Once back in our daily routine will that calm emptiness sustain us? The meditative states that Zen provides are wonderful in themselves, but they are only the first step to true peace. The baptized person cleans and calms his soul for another reason. The Blessed Trinity, our three-personed God, lives in our souls. But God goes unnoticed and unattended because of the clutter within. And so, when a Christian meditates it is to find the source of all peace, the God who dwells within. Recognizing and rejoicing in this loving Presence is the treasure we need to find. For this reason we meditate not simply to empty ourselves, but to be filled with the awareness of God. Not only have we found our inner calm, but we have connected with the very Source and Goal of our existence.

I have surely composed and calmed my spirit
as a weaned child, resting on its mother;
like a weaned child, so is my spirit in me. (Ps 131:2)

And you

Calm and peace of mind result from reflection. The routine of life continues on. We still have the concerns of jobs, study, family, health, finance, friendship, politics, and many more. We cannot easily dispose of them, nor do we want to; they are the reference points of our life. Meditation and prayer give us the calm to endure and the energy to go on. God is with us in our *now*. Do you rest in this awareness?

74

Friend or Faux?

Prayer

After confession, has the priest ever given you a two-part penance? The first part concerns the prayers to be said, but part two might startle us: *do an act of kindness for someone you've offended.*

Don't think of this as a double whammy! After all, you just went to confession as a sinner and came out forgiven. This double-decker penance contains a lot of wisdom. It causes us to speak humbly to God in prayer, and it lets us do something for him. Most of us try to make up for any offense we've given. Even if we don't say, "I'm sorry," we speak more kindly or offer some thoughtful gesture. It's a little trickier when we make up with God. We can pray reconciling words, but that's about it. We can't offer him a cup of coffee or give him a pat on the shoulder. The problem is that we can't see God.

Saint Augustine clarifies: "We may say, *But I haven't seen God.* However, one can't say, *I haven't seen men (or women).*

147

They can be loved and served. If we show love to those we see, we're also loving the One we can't see" (Commentary on the Letter of John, 5, 7).

How are these two—God and human beings—connected? Very simply. God used humanity as his trump card. In times past people wouldn't stay on the same page with him. They were forever wandering off or storming out on him, thinking him too demanding. At last God said: the time is right to send my Son. Through the cooperation of a human mother, God's Son was incarnate, that is, he became human. Why? To set things straight between God and us through his redemptive death, but also to give an example of how to live. In Jesus, God made himself our ultimate Friend, companion, and model. And so we follow his lead. We show God our desire for reconciliation by the way we treat others. In a real sense, we're incarnating our act of contrition: *Let me show you, God, how much I love you.*

> *May the Lord cause you to increase and overflow with love for one another and for everyone, . . . to strengthen your hearts to be blameless in holiness before our God and Father. (1 Th 3:12–13)*

And you

The question remaining is this: Am I a friend or *faux* to Jesus, real or just pretend? Think of how you treat your friends. Are you as true with Jesus?

75

Taken for Granite

Prayer

No one wants to be known for having a stone-cold heart. To be rock solid, yes, but not stone cold! The many statues of our great ones seem to contest this. Nearly every city park has a noble hero astride a horse. Statues of saints and sinners adorn churches and museums. Outside sports arenas, great players are immortalized in motion. Some folks even felt compelled to have a statue erected over their graves. All these statues were cast in metal or carved in stone. Although the monuments are meaningful, we have little relationship with these figures.

We form our relationships with living, breathing, life-giving individuals. This is exactly what Jesus offers us in the Blessed Sacrament, or the Real Presence. In human relationships we cherish those that encompass both our body and soul. A meaningful relationship is a mutual gift of one whole person to another. When the bread is consecrated at Mass,

Jesus takes over the substance of that bread. It becomes his ingenious way of remaining present with us. Always Jesus is really present this way in the church's tabernacle. Many people feel drawn to spend time with the Real Presence, speaking with Jesus, confiding in him, begging for blessings. To accommodate this desire the Church allows for time of adoration. Jesus, hidden within the appearance of the sacramental bread, is placed in a large ornate display called a monstrance, where the Sacred Host can be seen in a glass window.

During times of adoration those present may pray an hour of adoration together. This usually consists of readings, prayers, and hymns shared aloud. Adoration can also be done alone. Whenever the church is open, we can come in to spend time with Jesus.

> As Jesus gazed upon him [the rich young man] he was moved with love for him and said, "One thing is left for you; go sell what you have and give to the poor and you'll have treasure in Heaven, and come follow me." (Mk 10:21)

And you

Jesus is one Person who delights in spontaneous, unplanned visits. Any time you pass a church, check the door. If it opens, drop in for at least a moment or two.

What if I have nothing to say? That's the perfect way to begin a relationship. Just come in and shyly keep Jesus company. Eventually one of you will have something to say.

76

Can a Sinner Pray?

Prayer

Have you ever watched a dog chase its tail? It is totally intent on pursuing itself. Around and around it goes, unaware that the end is near. From our perspective it's a useless endeavor. Living in sin is something like this. Living in sin creates a self-centered existence. It is all about me: first my pleasure, then my pursuit, then my self-preservation, until I am brought up with nothing but my final end in sight

Sin is a kind of vortex. At first a single sin seems harmless enough. We suffer no noticeable consequences, but one sin turns into two sins, then three sins—until soon enough we find ourselves chasing our tails, so to speak. We have fallen into a pattern that will swirl on endlessly until it sucks us into an impossible situation.

To break the cycle, the dog needs a pat on the head; the sinner needs the touch of grace.

Dogs chase their tails because they think it is something other than themselves. They don't have the power of reflection. We humans do have the power to reflect, not just on what we are doing, but on ourselves as we do it. When we are intent on sinning, we try to ignore this ability to reflect. Although we think we have outwitted ourselves, it cannot be done. Later on, our reflection kicks in, often with a vengeance. We then suffer constant self-recrimination, a guilty conscience, a distrust of self, and a fear of punishment. Perhaps we even go as far as Adam and Eve after their tragic sin and try to hide from God. All we need is humility. All we need to do is admit our sin and ask the Lord for forgiveness. Can a sinner pray? In reality, it is the only thing a sinner can do, and it is the one thing a sinner must do.

"I'll get up and go to my father and I'll say to him, 'Father, I've sinned against Heaven and before you.'" (Lk 15:18)

And you

Remember you are not the only person who ever sinned. We all sin from time to time, unfortunately. The blessing in it is that God is always waiting to forgive us.

The First Date

Prayer

Is this you at prayer? "I feel like I'm talking to no one about nothing!" If so, you must be pretty pathetic on a first date. Yes, prayer is much like a date. We may not want to ask outright, but we certainly hope our date feels some kind of connection and finds us attractive.

In prayer it is God who sits across from us at the table of life. He is thinking: "Does this person feel any connection with me? Does this beautiful creation of mine find anything about me attractive?"

How do we turn our blank stare into prayer? Certainly this requires some effort and creativity: a bit of the mind, a bit more of the heart, and a sizable chunk of desire. Come to prayer, as you would to a date, with some of your best ice-breakers: "So glad you're here; you look lovely; what's your line of work? I'm an only child. How about you?" At the beginning you may feel a little foolish, but you will find an exchange takes place. You feel a little warmth, a spark in your heart.

Remember that relationships have to develop. They grow with time. So, between prayer dates, read the book God wrote (the Bible) and talk about God to people who know him well. Soon enough you will find yourself dreaming of the life you will make together.

Good relationships require more than superficial attraction, and so it is in prayer. Put in the necessary effort to keep yourself engaged in prayer. Meditate on what interests God: the good of all people, their salvation, and the maintenance of the universe. Discuss what is in your heart: your needs, your concerns about your family, the future, about how to live in these confusing times.

We know and believe in the love God has for us. God is love, and whoever abides in love abides in God, and God abides in him. (1 Jn 4:16)

And you

God is always the perfect date: attentive, engaged. What kind of date are you? Putting the effort into prayer means centering all of your attention on the Lord. He is the Someone who is interested in everything you have to say.

78

Happy Returns

Prayer

It's restaurant night! Hooray! No cooking, no cleanup: life is perfect—at least tonight. The meal exceeds our expectations and, as the bill is prepared, we pack leftovers in cardboard containers. A happy task: we will enjoy the feast again tomorrow.

This is the feeling we should take from Sunday Mass. It is the big feast of prayer where everything served is so abundant that we take away leftovers that last us throughout the coming week. What are these takeaways?

There is the sense of belonging to something larger than ourselves. Baptism makes us members of the Church and binds us into the Body of Christ. Pray that this oneness as family stays with us.

We also bring away thoughts from the Scripture readings and our priest's homily. These are words of the One who cares most about us, words to hold on to and pray over.

We have our shared concerns spoken as intercessions. During the week we can pray for the needs of each person who was there.

The moment of consecration is when the bread and wine are changed into the Body and Blood of Christ the Lord. This is the holiest, most important moment on earth, and we were there. When we receive the wafer or host, now Christ's Body, and the wine, now Christ's Blood, we are the most privileged persons on earth. Return to this moment and relive it in love and awe. This is how much our God wants to be with us, to be part of our lives. He humbles himself completely, to the point of simply being our food and drink, to sustain us on our journey, to be that close to us. This seems unbelievable, but we do believe it.

> *For my flesh is true food,*
> *And my blood is true drink.*
> *Whoever feeds on my flesh and drinks my blood*
> *Remains in me, and I in him. (Jn 6:55–56)*

And you

Don't be overwhelmed. As Christians, we are living in the mystery of God's loving plan. The secret is humility. Never shy away thinking you're unworthy. Jesus, the Second Person of the Blessed Trinity, practiced humility in coming to live our human life. And rather than abandon us at his death and resurrection, he decided to remain with us in the Blessed Sacrament. A humble act for a man, but how much more so for God. Be unashamed to humbly return his love.

Life-Giving Faith

Prayer

How impressive to witness the Gentleman Jesus curse a fig tree. "May no one ever eat fruit from you ever again!" he said (Mk 11:14). The tree immediately shriveled up. What caused such embarrassment for this poor tree? Lack of fruit! That was it! The tree had nothing to offer the hungry traveler. Was it fig season, you ask? According to Mark's Gospel it was. The companions of Jesus asked him to explain He answered with a lesson on prayer. Not just a tree, Jesus declared, but also a mountain will obey a word said with faith. "Therefore, I say to you, whatever you pray for and ask for, believe that you've received it and it will be yours," Jesus promised (Mk 11:24).

When we are not producing fruit, that is, not getting results from our efforts, the cause is often tepidity. "Tepidity" brings to mind tepid water, so disappointing when we are expecting a nice tall glass of cold water, or when we hope for a steaming cup of tea. Jesus said of tepid people that he would spit them out (see Rev 3:15–16). He expects us to make the effort to pray well, to be good, honest people, to make at least our little corner of earth a better place.

Tepidity is a virus of the spirit that sets us up for failure: doubts, disorientation, unhappiness. How terrible! Life is too short to be spent in lukewarmness. Shake off that inattentiveness, throw yourself into some activity that will stimulate a little faith, then pray and ask Jesus for the blessing of new life. Even the sighting of tiny new leaves means the fruit is near.

Fight the good fight of faith, seize the eternal life to which you were called when you nobly professed your faith before many witnesses. (1 Tm 6:12)

And you

Grab some for yourself today! This slogan is often used for selling products or services. Somehow grabbing sounds aggressive, but the intention is for the buyer to seize the opportunity offered. Jesus wants you to seize onto faith. Can you pray with confidence, believing that God will answer your prayer? Pray to be a person of strong faith, a tree that bears much fruit. Jesus offers a new life, a purposeful life, a life that bears fruit in holiness, goodness, and truth. You must take the opportunities he offers by living the life of a believer.

Are We There Yet?

Prayer

We each have a fair supply of talents. One that I missed out on, however, is a sense of direction. I can get to certain places on my own, but for new locations I need maps and computer-generated directions. I do know that having the ocean on my right on the East Coast means I'm headed north, and if the ocean's on my right on the West Coast I'm going south. Pretty basic stuff. But now, at the end of our book, we might ask about prayer: Are we there yet? Am I at least going in the right direction?

Without a second thought I would say yes, you are doing well. You have waded through a lot of prayer talk, and you have made some forays into your own prayer life. On the journey of prayer we all travel at our own speed. We use the means best for us, and our routes may differ as well. But it is the trip that matters, not the means. We will not reach our destination too early or too late. Prayer is, after all, only the journey, the travel. Prayer is leading us to our heavenly home. Prayer is, of itself, the right route.

Sometimes it is best to "go with the flow," as we might do in heavy traffic. Join in the group recitation of prayer, go with the cadence of the group, and reflect on the prayers you are sharing. At other times you might seek an alternate route, perhaps enjoying something you haven't experienced before.

So, when charting your prayer life, remember prayer isn't the end, it's not the destination. No, we are not there yet, but we are on our way as we pray.

> [Jesus said to them]: "Whatever you ask the Father for in my name he'll give you. Up till now you've asked for nothing in my name; ask and you'll receive, so your joy may be complete." (Jn 16:23–24)

And you

As you took this journey into prayer, which types of prayer appealed more to you? Are you more comfortable talking with God now? Do you join more willingly in prayer with others, especially in the celebration of Mass? All of us struggle with prayer; all of us have our ups and downs, but remember that God is a very good listener and our closest Friend.

Appendix

Prayers

The Lord's Prayer (Our Father)

Our Father, who art in heaven, hallowed be thy name; thy kingdom come, thy will be done on earth as it is in heaven. Give us this day our daily bread, and forgive us our trespasses, as we forgive those who trespass against us. And lead us not into temptation, but deliver us from evil. Amen.

Hail Mary

Hail Mary, full of grace, the Lord is with you. Blessed are you among women, and blessed is the fruit of your womb, Jesus. Holy Mary, Mother of God, pray for us sinners now and at the hour of our death. Amen.

Glory Be

Glory be to the Father, and to the Son, and to the Holy Spirit, as it was in the beginning, is now, and ever shall be, world without end. Amen.

Angel of God

Angel of God, my guardian dear, to whom God's love entrusts me here, ever this day be at my side to light and guard, to rule and guide. Amen.

Morning Offering

O Jesus, through the Immaculate Heart of Mary, I offer you my prayers, works, joys, and sufferings of this day, for all the intentions of your Sacred Heart, in union with the Holy Sacrifice of the Mass throughout the world, in reparation for my sins, for the intentions of all my relatives and friends, and in particular for the intentions of the Holy Father. Amen.

Prayer to Saint Michael

Saint Michael the Archangel, defend us in battle. Be our protection against the wickedness and snares of the devil. May God rebuke him, we humbly pray, and may you, O prince of the heavenly hosts, by the power of God, cast into hell Satan and all the evil spirits, who prowl about the world seeking the ruin of souls. Amen.

Apostles' Creed

I believe in God,
the Father almighty,
Creator of heaven and earth,
and in Jesus Christ, his only Son, our Lord,
(Here we bow until after the words "the Virgin Mary.")
who was conceived by the Holy Spirit,
born of the Virgin Mary,
suffered under Pontius Pilate,
was crucified, died and was buried;
he descended into hell;
on the third day he rose again from the dead;
he ascended into heaven,
and is seated at the right hand of God the Father
    almighty;
from there he will come to judge the living and the dead.
I believe in the Holy Spirit,
the holy catholic Church,
the communion of saints,
the forgiveness of sins,
the resurrection of the body,
and life everlasting. Amen.

Divine Praises

Blessed be God.
Blessed be his holy Name.
Blessed be Jesus Christ, true God and true man.

Blessed be the Name of Jesus.

Blessed be his most Sacred Heart.

Blessed be his most Precious Blood.

Blessed be Jesus in the most holy Sacrament of the altar.

Blessed be the Holy Spirit, the Paraclete.

Blessed be the great Mother of God, Mary most holy.

Blessed be her holy and Immaculate Conception.

Blessed be her glorious assumption.

Blessed be the name of Mary, Virgin and Mother.

Blessed be Saint Joseph, her most chaste spouse.

Blessed be God in his angels and in his saints.

Renewal of Baptismal Promises

I renew my baptismal promises: Once again I reject Satan. I reject all his works. I reject all his empty promises. I believe in God, the Father almighty, Creator of heaven and earth. I believe in Jesus Christ his only Son, our Lord, who was born of the Virgin Mary; who was crucified, died and was buried; who rose from the dead and is now seated at the right hand of the Father. I believe in the Holy Spirit, the holy Catholic Church, the communion of saints, the forgiveness of sins, the resurrection of the body, and life everlasting.

The Joyful Mysteries

1. The Annunciation—Mary becomes the Mother of God

2. The Visitation—Mary visits Saint Elizabeth

3. The Nativity—Jesus is born in a stable in Bethlehem

4. The Presentation of Jesus in the Temple—Mary and Joseph present Jesus to God

5. The Finding of Jesus in the Temple—Mary and Joseph find Jesus talking about God his Father

The Mysteries of Light

1. The Baptism of Jesus—John baptizes Jesus

2. The Wedding at Cana—Jesus works his first miracle

3. Jesus Announces God's Kingdom—Jesus teaches the people to turn their hearts to God

4. The Transfiguration—Jesus shines with the glory of God

5. Jesus Gives Us the Holy Eucharist—Jesus offers us his Body and Blood as food to make us strong in love and holiness

The Sorrowful Mysteries

1. The Agony in the Garden—Jesus suffers and prays

2. The Scourging at the Pillar—Jesus is tied up and whipped

3. The Crowning with Thorns—The soldiers make fun of Jesus
4. The Carrying of the Cross—Jesus carries his heavy cross
5. The Crucifixion—Jesus is nailed to the cross and dies for us

The Glorious Mysteries

1. The Resurrection—Jesus rises from the dead
2. The Ascension—Jesus goes back to heaven
3. The Descent of the Holy Spirit—The Holy Spirit comes down upon Mary and the apostles
4. The Assumption—Mary is taken body and soul to heaven
5. The Coronation—Mary is crowned Queen of heaven and earth

Index of Themes

Joseph, 20
Judas, 65

kingdom of God, 62

last judgment, 18
love, 74, 77
lukewarmness, 79

martyrdom, 40
Mary, 39
Mary Magdalene, 71
Mass, 16, 58, 59, 75, 78, 80
mature prayer, 47
meditation, 73, 77
mercy, 64
Michael, 30
mind, will, heart, 27
morning prayer, 43
mothers, 39
mystery, 4

name of God, 31, 61
news, praying the, 52

parish prayer, 51
patience, 6
peace of mind, 73
Penance, 74

BOOKS & MEDIA

A mission of the Daughters of St. Paul

As apostles of Jesus Christ, evangelizing today's world:

We are CALLED to holiness
by God's living Word and Eucharist.

We COMMUNICATE the Gospel message
through our lives and through all
available forms of media.

We SERVE the Church
by responding to the hopes and needs
of all people with the Word of God,
in the spirit of St. Paul.

For more information visit our website: www.pauline.org.

BOOKS & MEDIA

The Daughters of St. Paul operate book and media centers at the following addresses. Visit, call or write the one nearest you today, or find us at www.pauline.org..

CALIFORNIA

3908 Sepulveda Blvd, Culver City, CA 90230	310-397-8676
935 Brewster Avenue, Redwood City, CA 94063	650-369-4230
5945 Balboa Avenue, San Diego, CA 92111	858-565-9181

FLORIDA

145 S.W. 107th Avenue, Miami, FL 33174	305-559-6715

HAWAII

1143 Bishop Street, Honolulu, HI 96813	808-521-2731

ILLINOIS

172 North Michigan Avenue, Chicago, Il 60601	312-346-4228

LOUISIANA

4403 Veterans Memorial Blvd, Metairie, LA 70006	504-887-7631

MASSACHUSETTS

885 Providence Hwy, Dedham, MA 02026	781-326-5385

MISSOURI

9804 Watson Road, St. Louis, MO 63126	314 965 3512

NEW YORK

64 W. 38th Street, New York, NY 10018	212-754-1110

SOUTH CAROLINA

243 King Street, Charleston, SC 29401	843-577-0175

TEXAS

Currently no book center; for parish exhibits or outreach evangelization, contact: 210–488–4123 or SanAntonio@paulinemedia.com

VIRGINIA

1025 King Street, Alexandria, VA 22314	703-549-3806

CANADA

3022 Dufferin Street, Toronto, ON M6B 3T5

¡También somos su fuente para libros,
videos y música en español!